D1327590

JOURNEY UNDER THE
SOUTHERN STARS

Journey under the Southern Stars

by

E. L. GRANT WATSON

Illustrated with photographs

Abelard-Schuman

LONDON   NEW YORK   TORONTO

Other books by the same author

ANIMALS IN SPLENDOUR   THE MYSTERY OF PHYSICAL LIFE
ENIGMAS OF NATURAL HISTORY   THE PARTNERS
MORE ENIGMAS   THE NUN AND THE BANDIT

> TO MY GRANDSON HUGH SPENCE
> THAT HE MAY KNOW WHAT THE WORLD
> WAS ONCE LIKE

© E. L. Grant Watson
First published 1968

Library of Congress Catalogue Card Number 68. 13561
Standard Book Number 200 71529 1

LONDON   NEW YORK   TORONTO
Abelard-Schuman   Abelard-Schuman   Abelard-Schuman
Limited   Limited   Canada Limited
8 King Street WC2   6 West 57 Street   896 Queen Street West

Contents

Illustrations

ONE

The Voyage Out

— ★ —

MORE THAN FIFTY YEARS AGO I was offered a place as zoologist in a small expedition to northwest Australia, consisting of A. R. Brown* and myself, and later a Swedish sailor called Louis Olsen. Brown, who had been at Trinity College, Cambridge, planned to study the marriage customs of the aborigines. He had made his name as an anthropologist on an expedition to the Andaman Islands in 1906. The lower island was at this time unexplored and was reputed to be inhabited by cannibals. Brown, accompanied only by his cook, made contact with the cannibals and within a short time had established himself as ruler of the island. When he returned to Cambridge in 1908, he was made a Fellow of Trinity College. His imperious manner, however, did not recommend him in a donnish society, and I was strongly advised not to go with him. But I was willing to follow his lead, and we got on very well.

My appointment would carry no salary, and I would have to pay my own expenses, but I could sell whatever I collected. I was already known to two eminent collectors of insects; one offered to pay me ten shillings for twenty specimens of any and every kind of beetle, and I could name my own price for any I considered rare. The other specialized in fleas, and he paid a

---

*Alfred Radcliffe-Brown, 1881–1955. Professor of Social Anthropology in several universities, his important contributions in the field dealt mainly with the establishment of a systematic framework of social structure in simple societies.

pound for twelve fleas of any species. This sounded easy, but fleas are difficult to catch, so the prospect was not financially brilliant.

Berths were booked on S.S. *Suevic*, an old White Star liner that went to Australia via the Cape. A few weeks before sailing, Brown had to postpone his departure for private reasons, and I decided to go alone and pick up some sort of job to keep myself until Brown joined me.

Liverpool in the early morning looked dreary with rain falling through an east wind. The day was a Friday, the thirteenth of January, 1910, but I considered myself above superstitious qualms. The sea was choppy even in the harbour, and the old *Suevic* lay a good way out from the land, a long narrow boat with a reputation of not being a roller, though she was said to pitch a good deal. Cold and miserable, I and my companions clambered up the boarding-ladder from the tug; and what a crowd of dismal human creatures we appeared to one another!

The preliminary formalities accomplished, I went to look at my cabin. It was a good-sized room, and I was glad to see a large port-hole opposite my berth. It was, however, screwed down. No chance of it being opened, I was told, until we were off the African coast. A notice, *No Smoking Allowed*, figured large, but this was ignored after the first day. The atmosphere was soon pretty thick, and remained so for the first two weeks, since the weather was rough and the only ventilation was through a passage permeated with the odours of the men's lavatory.

I looked with interest and some anxiety at my companions. There were two bricklayers, pleasant fellows who never once during the whole voyage took off their clothes. They slept in them, and had no such refinements as tooth-brushes. There was a humorous little Scotsman who had been a printer, and an enormous man who soon acquired the nickname of Tiny. There was the younger son of Pink, of jam-making fame, a tough, reliable young fellow who became my friend and adviser; a dark-haired youth who was out to seek his fortune in the New World; two other rather undistinguished individuals, and a middle-aged sportsman with an enormous collection of sticks and umbrellas.

With some interest I watched him bestow all these in his bunk and cover them up with his blanket. It later transpired that he was a kleptomaniac, and these were the fruits of his activities at Liverpool station, and on the train. During the first few weeks he was merely a nuisance, collecting things from all over the ship, and hiding them in his bunk. If anything was lost, we knew where to look; but later, when the weather became hot, he was found clambering over the side of the ship, clutching a life-belt, prepared to swim his way home. He was rescued, fighting like the madman he was, and was then confined in a miserable little box of a place just over the screw. He had been put on board by his loving family with a ticket to Brisbane. At Brisbane, as I heard later, he was not allowed to land, but was sent back.

It took time to get accustomed to the mid-ship atmosphere, and to the bugs, of which there was no lack. On lifting out the wooden sides of my bunk, which fitted into iron slots, I discovered the lurking-place of these hemiptera, where they clustered in scores and could be easily burnt by the application of a match. The vitiated atmosphere was more difficult to accommodate oneself to, but one can grow accustomed to most things, and once asleep, I fell into a deep and not unpleasant coma. On waking up, there was always available a hot sea bath. These baths I much enjoyed, especially when the water was full of phosphorescent organisms which left my body outlined in faint and delicate silver. An early walk on deck in the fresh ocean air dispelled the coma of the night.

When we passed Finisterre, we came into warm sunny weather and calm seas, and when we sighted Tenerife I shall never forget my vision of its mountain cap of snow, rising above the clouds and seeming to float in the sky: a marvel of loveliness, a thing to take away the breath and make the heart miss a beat.

I was delighted by the tropical seas, and the warm, delicious winds. On the surface of the ocean floated Portuguese men-of-war, pink and blue and white, and over the surface from time to time skimmed flying fish. There were shoals of porpoises, iridescent in a hundred colours, and more than once we sighted whales.

My fellow-travellers I found a great deal nicer than my first impression had led me to suppose. We had the run of the greater part of the big ship, which was a staunch sea-boat, though thoroughly dirty. The food, considering our low passage money, was good, but most things partook of the overwhelming aroma of the galley. The drinking water was flat, and had a sickly flavour.

Apart from such minor drawbacks, life renewed itself in wonder; Halley's comet was a marvel to behold. Each night as we fared southward, its bending arc above us grew greater and grander. Its head appeared about a fifth the size of the moon, and its tail was a vast translucent veil, spreading out over an enormous arc. An awesome sight; night after night I would stand on the upper deck star-gazing, and delighting in the soft tropical air and the sound of water as it swished along the sides of the ship. The mixed noises of the hum of engines, the tumult of the screws, the dance-music, the banging and the bumping which always accompanies the life of a ship, the clank and ringing of bells, the calls of human voices: these all added to that complex human achievement which is an ocean liner.

After we had left the Cape and were sidling our way southwards towards the "roaring forties" the scene was very different from the serene West African ocean. The world, though still only the world of waters, was revealed in other moods. Here the *Suevic* furrowed her course through increasingly large waves, which lifted her stern so high that the ship seemed to stand on her head. A constant spume of water swept the decks, and we, who still walked there, must climb the rising hillside, or clutch at a railing while the declivity increased at our feet.

The climate was cold and exhilarating, often rainy, though there were sometimes clear skies at night when the map of starry heavens swung above our heads. Moments of happiness came as I clutched a stanchion, and watched the skies spin round, and saw the ship's lights fade into the night. I watched the following albatrosses, whose flight was so much more powerful and swift than that of the ship. On seemingly motionless wings, one of these great birds would hang a few yards from the masthead; then, with the least movement, it would slope away to grow faint in the distance and be lost, only to reappear as calm and as motionless as before.

From such vantage it could survey the whole length of the labouring liner, and when the galley-scuttle opened and refuse was shot forth, it would swoop to the waves and be left behind, appearing again a few minutes later at the same point of vantage.

When watching an albatross one might I had my first experience of being really and completely alone. A middling sea was running, big waves from time to time lifted the stern; the propellers raced in a spume of bubbles. We were making the "roaring forties" somewhere southeast of the Cape, following the curve of the world. Beneath me was the unceasing urge of the engines and all around, farther than I could see, the grey indifferent waters.

As I gazed at the turbulent eddies, up-swirling and down-twisting, being beaten into foam by our passage, the thought came—whether I died tonight or forty years hence, should I not be lost in just such an eternal ocean? These planks, these iron plates that bore me up and carried me along towards a destination that was only a name, became unsubstantial and the sight of the sea grew so terrible that I could not look any longer. I climbed the ladder to the boat deck, where I should not be so close to the waves.

Overhead was a sky of unusual splendour, for at that time Halley's comet was at its full magnificence. Each night since we had left England, I had watched it growing bigger and rising higher; now it crossed the zenith. The enormous tail sprayed out in the faintest transparent veil, and distant stars shone through.

For a good ten days, we were in the region of high seas and gales, as the eastward-flowing currents helped us on our way. Then, as we sloped northeast, the weather became less boisterous and excitement grew among us, for Australia would be sighted, and, for some few of us, the sea journey accomplished; now with the anticipation of the new adventure on a new continent was mingled regret at the partings which were so near.

That first journey from Albany to Perth, mild as the occupation of gazing out of a window would seem, was an adventure. Paper-trees with stumpy, ragged stems growing in the swamps near Albany, the long-haired casuarinas and scrubby eucalyptus, grevilleas of many kinds, and the host of flowering herbs were all unlike the English scene. The sound of bull-frogs croaking in the swamps could clearly be heard at the station halts. The abandoned cries of the kookaburra and the cawing of the reddish-black crows, the song of the cicadas and the hum of innumerable insect wings offered a foretaste of the new land.

Perth, a city with trams, shops and overhead wires, had much in common with all modern towns, but was distinguished by a public park set on a hill above the city. Everywhere I looked was delight in novelty; the crimson rosettes of the flowering eucalyptus and the shaving-brush tufts of the melanenca, the strange black blossoms of kangaroo's paws were all close at hand, and in the distance the city roofs under brilliant sunshine. The blue of Perth water was flecked by flocks of birds; pelicans as wild and almost as common as seagulls, black swans which, when they flew, revealed the pinkish-scarlet of under-wings, innumerable lesser birds, ducks and gulls, whose names I did not know.

I had come charged with good resolutions to earn my keep from the start, but the temptation to look and absorb was too strong. I would remain free for another week at any rate, and so booked a room at St. George's coffee-palace where I was fed on new kinds of sea-fish, on turkey and fruit and cream. During this time I made the acquaintance of Mr. Giles, the keeper of wild animals at Perth Zoological Gardens. Giles was one of those humans whom animals seem to recognize as mystically allied to themselves. He could enter the cages of the most dangerous wild beasts, and they would not hurt him. Even with camels he was on friendly terms. Camels were used for drawing the great wagons loaded with wool from the interior of the northwest to the coastal towns. They were often to be seen in teams sixty strong, and whether they were lying down, chewing their interminable cud or blowing out those strange bladder-like bags which they harbour in their mouths, or standing, walking or kneeling, their necks were very much longer than they seemed. Often I have started back in alarm as a camel's magnificently formidable denture has snapped within an inch of my nose, and an odoriferous breath has enveloped my face.

I had already started to collect insects, and before the week was up I had despatched my first tin of two thousand beetles. It was Giles who told me where to look for the rare longicorns whose females never emerge from the wood. These I found months afterwards on the upper reaches of the Gascoyne River. I priced them at twelve pounds each! I think now that I might have asked twenty for them, and perhaps more.

At the end of the week I decided to visit the goldfields, thinking that there, perhaps, I should tumble into a job. The West Australian government had generously offered to members of the expedition a first-class pass on the railways. Travelling would be no expense, and so, leaving my luggage at the coffee-palace, I set off in a first-class carriage on the night express for Kalgoorlie.

In the same carriage there were travelling four men. One, a tough-looking gentleman with a glass eye, proved to be the well-known Doree Doolette, mine-owner and company-promoter. With him was a disreputable-looking and infirm Irishman, and two other well-to-do Australians. No sooner had we left Perth station than they started playing poker for pound points. I watched while Doolette relieved his companions of more than eighty

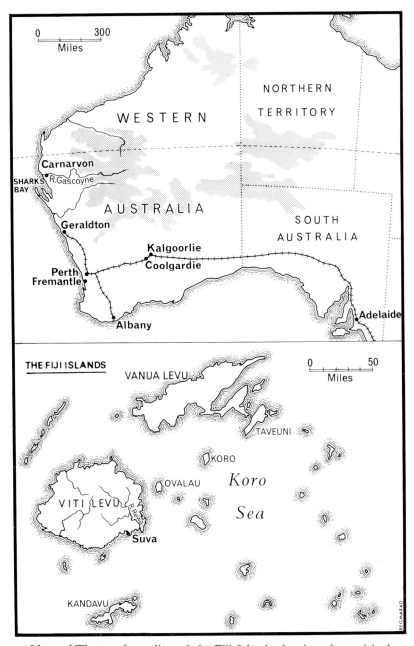

Maps of Western Australia and the Fiji Islands showing places visited
by the author

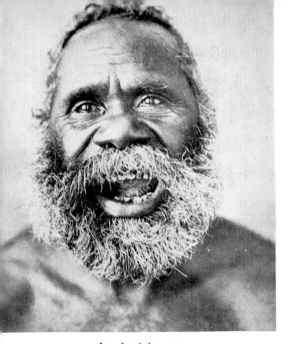

An aborigine man

Group of aborigines in the Australian bush

pounds. At Midland Junction two of the poker party left the train and Doolette and his Irish companion were alone with me.

He raised his one good eye questioningly, while his glass one glittered. Would I care for a little friendly game? I thanked my stars that I had left my fifty pounds banked in Perth, and only had a few sovereigns on me. These I clutched nervously, as I explained that I was a mere pauper, a member of a scientific expedition, and that all I hoped to do was to live inexpensively for the next few weeks and see what I could of the country. Doolette's manner changed. Would I like to see a gold mine? He was visiting a little mine in which he had interests, and would take me there, if I liked.

"Would it cost much?" I asked.

Nothing at all! I could come as his guest. He was going for a day to Kalgoorlie, but on the morrow would be returning to Southern Cross. From there we would drive into the bush. Would I care to come?

I remembered my mother's warning that the world was full of sharks waiting to eat pigeons. Here obviously was one of the greater sharks, and, in my corner, one of the pigeons. I said that I should like to come very much, but that I had very little money. He said I would not need to spend a penny; I had better buy some bush-clothes, dungarees and a singlet, and then, with a glance at my head, added, "Have a hair-cut".

In the early dawn, Kalgoorlie was excitingly attractive, a crisp air enveloping the huge dumps of powdered ores, which rose picturesquely from amongst the mine-superstructures. The roads were of the same powdered dust; its brick-red hue coloured everything. A great exhilaration was in the dry, high atmosphere.

Doolette went off to his expensive hotel, and I to find a coffee-palace. A cold bath, a good breakfast, and then for the exploration of the town, and for my fitting-up according to the national standard. First to the hairdresser's, then to buy singlet and dungarees, then back to the coffee-palace for the transformation.

The day I spent lounging in Kalgoorlie, becoming red with the dust of the goldfields, accustoming my eyes to the desert, arid landscape made barren by a blazing sun by day and dry frost by night. The city's water-supply was brought more than three hundred and fifty miles from the Mundaring Weir. In the midst of the town was a great garden of tropical luxuriance. This was the property of one of the big mine-owners and it was said he paid twenty pounds a week for the watering of his garden alone.

I met Doolette and his Irish friend at the station that evening, and we took the west-bound train for Southern Cross. Southern Cross was at that time little more than a wayside halt, or so it appeared at two o'clock in the morning. We alighted under a bright, frosty sky. A buggy, drawn by horses, was waiting for us. Doolette sat beside the driver and I beside the Irishman on the back seat. We started on the long cross-country drive to the Bulfinch, the new mine in which Doolette was interested. This was, of course, before the great boom, when the Bulfinch was merely a possibility, which might or might not be worth while; it was not yet the glittering fortune that eluded all but the few.

At first we followed a track, but soon were making our way across the wild bush-scrub. The going was not difficult since the mulga and acacia bushes did not grow close together, and it was easy to steer between them, though often we jolted over fallen stems. The wild beauty of the night, the blazing stars in the black sky, the steaming horses and the feathery and ghostly mulga bushes would have been sufficient company; but all the time Doolette's Irish friend poured out upon me a stream of dirty stories, and nudged me to make sure that I saw the point. Often I did not; often the point was very blunt.

The night air was bitterly cold and all the rugs and wraps that Doolette had provided did not seem enough to keep us warm; at last dawn came, and with it the sight of an increasing number of wheel-tracks making in the same direction.

Unexpectedly a voice singing the *Preislied* from the *Meistersinger* came to me, and in a few moments we had drawn up on the outskirts of the Bulfinch camp. Men came to greet us, among them Jim Wickham, the overseer, who had been singing the *Preislied*. He was a steady, firm Englishman, who knew his own worth.

Soon we were sitting on upturned boxes round a camp-fire eating large portions of eggs and bacon and mutton chops, together with thick chunks of damper,* washed down by strong tea. A few salmon-gums in the distance raised their fan-shaped branches against the morning sky, but otherwise there was no feature to break the monotony of mulga and mallee scrub.

Doolette, whatever his relation with business rivals may have been, treated me with great generosity, and gave me of the camp's

---

* Unleavened cake baked in wood ashes.

hospitality, even providing me with a private tent. He himself did not stay long at the mine, but after a short inspection departed with his Irish friend, promising that he would be back soon. In the meanwhile, I could stay as long as I liked and collect beetles, or follow any other eccentricity.

Those first weeks in the desert bush were rich, not so much in outer as in inner experience. Outwardly, they soon presented a very pleasant and happy monotony. The waking at early dawn in bitter cold, the relished breakfast, as close to the camp-fire as I could squeeze, together with Jim Wickham and his men. About twenty men were at work. These all extended to me, and to my ignorance of bush ways, a kindly tolerance, though they were always telling me tall stories to see how much I would swallow. I amused myself by seeing how much I could make them believe that I believed of the stuff they told me. They discovered my simple artifice and were amused at my defence. They found amusement too in my activities, and in their times off would go hunting echidnas, or bush porcupines, which lived in hollows of fallen trees. The miners also brought me beetles and every kind of insect from mantis and phasmid to grasshoppers and crickets and ant-lions. I spent a great deal of my time collecting the thousands of beetles that lurked under the loose bark of the gum trees, or those I could so easily beat from the low bushes into my Bignal beating-tray. I wandered solitary in the bush, but never very far from a wheel-track, for I had a keen apprehension of how easy it would be to get lost.

By ten o'clock the climate was so far changed that sweaters were discarded. By eleven the sun was scorching hot, and at noon it was best to keep under cover. I was soon sunburnt, and my nose took on the appearance of a bright red blister. In the afternoon one could wander again, and at sundown was glad to pull on sweaters while the evening meal was in preparation.

When Doolette returned he was shown the samples of ore-dust from the borings. Great was his excitement when these were washed out under his one critical eye; "Holy Jesus," he exclaimed, "the bloody dish is full of gold!" He stayed on to superintend further borings and blastings, and each day washed out more samples. Soon it got round that here, at the Bulfinch, was something exceptional. Men began to drift in, and claims were staked anywhere near the original holding, which was shared between Doolette with seven-eighths, and his prospector with an eighth.

At the end of the week, Doolette offered me the job of washing and assessing samples, keeping a record for his private eye; he paid me what seemed a handsome sum for work which occupied so little of my time.

The mine when I first saw it was a shaft that went down twenty feet in the reddish-yellow rock. At its base was a short traverse. The men worked at a winch lifting buckets of ore, others were in the traverse, and others might vaguely be described as "fossicking around" at shallow outcrop workings. There was a rumour of a rich spray of gold in the quartz and orthoclase but one could never tell. For my part I looked at that dusty burrow from the distance of my great inexperience; I had not come to Australia to hunt for gold.

Chance and good fortune had brought me to this remote spot, and at that first impact my attention was absorbed by the pervading aura of a land as yet innocent of human exploitation. The red dust of decaying granite, bare of all but the scantiest herbs, the brittle-stemmed, blue-leaved mulga bushes which grew so far apart and seemed to have been there since the beginning of time, the occasional salmon-gums with their gracefully formed branches—these were untouched by man's presence on the earth. The unsullied background was lovely and aloof.

There was the mine, there were the men and all the camp activities, new and strange enough in themselves. After the first day, my insect-hunting led me progressively further into the bush, a great unknown that stretched for thousands of miles eastward. I was cautious, never leaving the cart-tracks that radiated this way or that, and breaking branches to show me the way I had come.

Two days after my arrival, a young engineer in government employ came out from Perth. His business was with the mine. "Bloody awful country, this," he remarked, and went on to talk of the gold and the rumours, then reverted to the awfulness of the country and the dust.

On the fourth day after his arrival he walked a couple of yards into the bush and shot himself. The comment in the camp was that he was not the first man that had done so under the influence of the bush. His blood-stained fly-clotted body, as it was found in the dust, appeared as both threat and warning. The episode was accepted simply as the sort of thing that happens, beyond explanation or remedy. The vacant place was taken by another man a few days later. Mildly grim jokes were made, suggesting that something of the kind might befall a mere beetle-hunting Johnnie from England. There was seriousness in the hint. I feared and was attracted to the bush, feeling a strange light-heartedness when alone, out of sight of my fellow men amidst the dry foliage of mulga, always the same, always silent and motionless under the sun's glare. The silence was made up of many occasional sounds: the croaking of the red-brown crows, the chatter of a passing flock of parakeets, the whirr of the wings of the blue and red locusts as they flew from bush to bush, and the continuous buzz of flies.

The mine developed, the bags of ore accumulated into heaps and were carried on wagons to the rail, thirty miles to the west. Men began to drift in; storekeepers, a pack of hungry profiteers, retailed blankets and food to a growing population. The prospecting fever grew, and rumours multiplied. Gold was twenty ounces to the ton, it was whispered; not twenty, a hundred, two hundred! No, far better; it was mullock held together by gold!

An immense intrusive dike of metamorphosed schist divided the granite plain. It was half a mile in width, and disappeared into the distance in either direction. Its presence was indicated by a slightly raised undulation. Through this dike, various veins of quartz and acid-rock made a network, and in these, or near them, clustered the sprays of gold. Those men who knew the metal might guess, and sometimes guess rightly, where the sprayings went.

In the fast-growing population were mingled the original workers of the mine and all those who had made secondary nearby claims. At the height of the boom these hit-or-miss chances went for thirty miles each way. With pick and shovel the men scratched trenches in the rock, ground their samples, and washed them, hoping for a "colour". Amongst all the men gathered in the vicinity were two who especially awakened my interest. There was the prospector, who in the first place had found the mine. He had an eighth share in whatever came out of it, and might already be considered a rich man. For the present his work was done, and he spent most of his time wandering by himself in the bush. Like the other men, he wore a singlet and blue dungarees, and was as dust-stained as the desert that was his home. He was shy of other men, and kept his face inclined towards the ground; he was lanky, yet supple and strongly built; his broad bronzed forehead was held forward as though to hide his sensitive mouth and chin. His swift glance, when he did raise his eyes, was not directed at his companion, but at the adjacent air. Often I would see him leaning against a tree in moody idleness, or sitting on a box, bent forward with elbows on knees, looking at his clasped hands. So he would remain for long periods, as though lost in inner cogitation. It was said of him that he could go anywhere in the bush and never be lost. He did not travel as most prospectors did, with cart and horse and a store of provisions and water, but went on foot with dolly and washing-pan and hammer, and dried fish in a tin. He found water as the natives did, often sucking it in a little tube from hollows in the rock. He found most of his food too, catching wallabies, bandicoots, lizards and snakes, and eating the large succulent caterpillars that lurked in the stems of acacias.

This man, I was told, knew more about gold and tin than any man in Western Australia. He could guess which way the sprays of gold were pointing, though they were deep underground. He could feel their unseen presence, as a diviner feels the presence of water. For many years he had followed the search, and men respected him for what he was, though they looked on him as odd, a peculiar fellow who only met them at his ease when he was drunk.

The other man was no less a slave of the bush magic, though of a different type. He was an elderly and exceedingly tough Irishman. When I first met him, he was working at a small claim he had staked on the outskirts of the camp. The gold from the ore he raised brought an average of five pounds a week. Nothing very good, but it might come better. And if it did? Well, it was always good to see the colour in the pan. Riches? He didn't want them. Money? He would send the money back to his wife in Dublin, whom he had not seen for some long and indefinite number of years. Her absence he did not regret, often declaring, with some salty remark, that sex was the curse of life. He loved the sight of the gold in the pan; that little wisp of yellow granules, like a microscopic comet's tail, mingled with the dark of ferromagnesium. He would never escape the bush this side of the grave, and had the intelligence to know it. Why should he want to escape? The life suited him well enough. "When you haven't washed for a month, you don't need ever to wash again," he told me.

Gilbert had been a brewer, and for reasons connected with his wife had left his native land. He was well-read. He drank no alcohol, and ate sparingly. He was as hard as an old mulga stem, and looked like one. His brilliant blue eyes seemed to look through the man he was talking to, to some far distant horizon. He was a witty talker and, like so many Irishmen, given to a picturesque exaggeration. In the camp he was considered a little mad, but he was the only man who could hold all the others silent, when in the evening he told his high-pitched tales to the gathering about the fire.

I was lucky in finding in him a friend and, for a short time, a partner. When the boom was at its height, everyone was infected with a general and communal intoxication. The glamour of the hidden treasure claimed us all, for the earth had revealed a hem of its gold vesture, and hundreds of men came pouring to the spot, staking their claims wildly and at hazard. One or two made fortunes, storekeepers flourished; but the great majority laboured and grew poorer than they had been. We all took partners in our hopeful searchings, and on all spare occasions we roamed the bush with hammers, to chip the outcrops and take samples to be dollied and washed, and eagerly scanned for the yellow dust. Gilbert, I think, was amused to talk with me, and to preach the philosophy of the curse of sex, to tell his tall stories, and, in his charity, to protect my obvious inexperience from the dangers of camp life. He took me as partner, and together we went prospecting. He led, and I followed.

Usually we would leave the great dike and set off across the granite plain to some small schistose intrusions that Gilbert knew of, and here we would stay alone for a day or two. He had a more permanent and more faithful partner than myself, a mongrel dog of medium size and large intelligence. With this dog, and carrying his axe and strong-smelling canister of dried fish, he would set out. I carried the water-bottles and other necessary gear. For a day or two we would be absent, living on the food we carried and rabbits the dog found in hollow tree-trunks. Trees had grown old and fallen in the long course of that endless bush-summer; their interiors had been eaten by ants. In these the rabbits lived. They did not burrow as in England, for the underlying granite was too hard. The dog sniffed at one end of a hollow log, then at the other, and, if the finding was good, he ran his nose along the outside, pausing at the place where the rabbit was crouching. We blocked the ends, and Gilbert split the log with his axe. Rabbits were easy

to catch and plentiful; boiled with salt fish they were not unaccept-
able to our hunger. We slept on the ground, wrapped in our
blankets, under starry skies.

During the night we had as close companions small bush
wallabies. These are nocturnal in habit, and quite fearless. They
came within a few feet of us, and often jumped over our sleeping
bodies. They were a distraction to our dog, who did not suffer
them quietly, but he soon learnt that he could not catch them and
contented himself with low growls of protest.

Our days began with the re-making of our fire, the cooking of
food, and the boiling of tea. We strayed at our fancy, as I and my
boyhood companion had strayed apart in the New Forest. I
always kept within call, careful not to lose my partner; of earth's
children, men only are easily lost, for they put themselves in
positions in which they can be lost, whereas animals seldom do.
Civilization has spoilt in men the sense of direction. The little
legless sand-lizards that disappear before the booted tread of a
man do not lose themselves, though they plunge into the dust like
eels wriggling through water. Most creatures know their places;
and the blue-winged, leaf-eating grasshoppers, though they
whirr away at random from their home-bushes, find other well-
suited bushes for their support.

Not only at night but during the day we had to avoid the ants,
which swarmed in many places, on the ground and often on bushes.
They were fierce, and could sting and bite. And we were shy of the
travelling armies of fleas. What these fleas were doing in the
desert, or how they were engendered, I never knew. We found
them hopping along in close-ranked battalions, hundreds and
thousands of them. They were hungry, indeed starving, and I
suppose they were marching blindly, impelled by hunger, to
chance on some blood-possessing creature. I have seen armies
lying dead and withered in the dust. Not only fleas perish in this
way; there are large numbers of ticks of various species that cling
by preference to the branches of dead bushes. Hanging by two
legs, with the other six legs they feel the air for any careless
creature that may pass; and since there are comparatively few
animals that do pass, whole bush-loads of ticks die of starvation
and wither away where they hang. It is remarkable that living
vegetation attracts certain kind of fauna, and that dead bushes
attract other species. Not only did we find ticks and ants with a
preference for dead bushes, but there were metallic-blue butter-

flies of the hairstreak tribe that perched on and clung to dead branches. I suspected that they had some kind of symbiosis with ants, though I did not discover what this was. Often I have seen dead thorn-bushes covered with the blue butterflies, some of them opening their metallically shining wings, others showing only the black undersides in the folded position. On the dead bushes they clung in hundreds, only a few visiting, on rare occasions, the living plants.

The majority of bush insects have protective colouring. The phasmids or stick-insects were the most remarkable of those we saw. These at their largest were eight to nine inches long, and had broad, pink wings which they only showed in flight; they kept them for the most part neatly folded over their backs and round their sides. At rest they exactly resembled the stems of the plants on which they lived, mimicking the nodes, the axillary buds and the twigs with great accuracy. There were many species, of all sizes. There were also many varieties of praying mantis, some when mature being little more than half an inch in length, some a good five inches long. All shared the same savage nature, the same insatiable hunger.

From short prospecting expeditions we would return to camp after a night or two's absence to discover an ever-increasing activity. Always more men, more dumps of stores, and a deeper, though always suppressed sense of excitement. The community of gold-hungry men generated its own atmosphere; yet, on the broad surface of that waste land, this human gathering was an insignificant biological eruption from which one could easily escape by walking a few hundred yards in any direction. At that time there had been no appreciable rainfall for more than eighteen months, and I was fortunate enough to witness the sudden break of this long dry spell. A week of heavy showers and brilliant sunny intervals brought an astonishing transformation. At the first impact of water on the red dust came that ravishing scent which rain always produces in contact with dry earth. A shallow layer of sticky mud soon covered the underlying dryness. Slowly this hardened into a more homogeneous mixture, pools appeared in the hollows, and all over the land sprang up, with amazing quickness, delicate green shoots from innumerable, unsuspected seeds. Within a few days flowers began to open. Most of these were small and elegant everlasting flowers with dry petals, some white, some pink and a few yellow, and all with a faint honey

scent resembling that of evening primroses. Thin-stemmed orchids with extravagant spidery petals stretched out brown-pink
blossoms. A climbing sundew twisted itself among the smaller
herbs, and all that had been parched and bare was soon a sweet-
scented carpet through which the more permanent blue foliage of
acacias, mulgas and casuarinas lifted in domes or cascades.

This springtime world was, in the act of astonishing resurrection,
populated with a vast increase of insect life, and creatures never
seen in the dry season made their appearance. Bees, wasps and
hover-flies of various kinds filled the air with buzzing, and the
winged males of a tribe known as the *Thindeae* hovered around
the flowers, carrying, as they flew, the wingless females clinging
to their bodies. The females were about a fifth of the size of the
males, and looked like ants; they were reputed to have a severe
sting, and were called by the miners "ant-cows".

Not only insects but all other creatures seemed miraculously to
increase. Lizards and snakes were far more numerous, and toads
unexpectedly made their appearance, twanging their hard-stringed
notes and disporting themselves wherever a little water gathered
into a shallow pool. These toads, I was told, lay buried in the dust
for as long as two years, if need be; when at last the rain came and
the earth was moistened, they pushed their way out for a short
gala period of eating and drinking and love-making. When the
sun dried up the water and burnt to dust the vegetation, they
made their way back into the earth again, to wait in somnolent
patience for the next rainfall.

The blossoming period did not last for long. The sun was a
scorching presence, turning back to dust all that the rain had
brought forth. After a few weeks nothing was left of the green
carpet and the gay blossoms. The granite of the plain looked as
though it could never have supported those fields of departed
flowers. Only the dry-stemmed, blue-leaved bushes remained, and
only those creatures that could live on very little moisture still
eked out a difficult existence. One of the most remarkable of these
was a little lizard about seven inches long, that was given the
misleading name of "mountain devil". Its appearance might, at a
stretch, be considered devilish, for its surface was drawn up into
a number of thorny spikes. These were neither for protection nor
for aggression, but served the purpose of increasing the surface.
On this extended surface of peaks and valleys, the little dew of the
desert could fall and pass direct through the spongy cuticle. This

was the source of its moisture. It did not drink, for there was no water, but a drop of water falling on its back disappeared as into blotting-paper. It ate small ants which it poked at with tortoise-like precision. I kept one or two of these little mountain devils tied by their tails to a tent-peg, and so was able to observe something of their habits. They were slow-moving helpless creatures, but strangely well adapted to the waterless condition of that inland bush.

Amongst this surrounding wild life was a vortex of human activity centred in the hope of riches. A few of the men, and certainly Gilbert among them, had a profound feeling for the bush. With Gilbert this feeling was identified with his search; it was not riches, or the hope of riches, that lured him on. It was the unknown background that held him in thrall, and the gold was the symbol of the impossible-to-realize centre of all life.

TWO

Life in the Bush

— ✳ —

WHEN BROWN ARRIVED we made preparations for a long sojourn in the bush. Our first task was to buy stores to take with us to the small up-rail town of Sandstone. From there we could go on with horse and cart to carry our camping outfit and drinking water in a big tank; for fresh meat, we must rely on what we shot.

Before we started, Brown gave a public lecture explaining our plans to make records of the marriage customs of those aborigines who had not, at that date, been in contact with white settlers. Brown was an exceptionally good lecturer, with a magic influence on his audience. Among those present was a wealthy sheep-farmer from the northwest. He came up after the lecture and asked whether we would accept a cheque of one thousand pounds to help us on our way. Brown thought it was a leg-pull, but accepted the cheque. The next day when presented at the bank, it was found to be perfectly good. This more than doubled our funds, and incidentally paid my expenses.

We travelled northward on a four-wagon train. The engine was driven by wood that had been stacked at stopping places beside the line, and at each stop all able-bodied men turned out to help fill the tender. We puffed and jerked northward through changing country, sometimes eucalyptus forest, sometimes over wastes of mallee and mulga scrub, sometimes beside salt lakes.

When we arrived at Geraldtown, our junction for the line that turned eastward towards the Murchison goldfields, it was early morning. The sun was already hot on the sandy soil, and on the squat houses which lay scattered in clusters like children's bricks kicked at random about the floor, crouched close to the ground, their roofs of corrugated iron painted dull red. Lines of pepper trees marked with dark and vivid green some future streets. Goats were nibbling at labels of discarded tin cans.

The hotel was the only two-storeyed building in the town, a square building with a central door opening on a passage that ran straight through a large room to another door on the far side. On the red divans men were lying, drinking or sleeping. Ancient decorations of coloured paper thick with dead flies adorned the ceiling. A great many live flies wove patterns between the dust-laden festoons. On the stairs, when we reached them, sprawled three drunken men whom we had to step over on the way to our room; we were fortunate to have a room to ourselves.

After a night of noisy festivities, we left on the inland railway for the small township of Sandstone where there was reported to be a gathering of the Australian tribes. This train was several grades more ramshackle than the one that had brought us from Perth; it seemed hardly an invention of the nineteenth century, but more like a prehistoric desert creature, very old, sun-dried and dusty, that had slunk from the inland uplands, and was now waiting to crawl back again to its native bush. It consisted of two coaches and a rusty engine. There were two so-called first-class compartments, and one of them had been reserved for Brown and myself. The only other people on the train were a company of noisy miners who occupied the third-class carriages.

We started at nine in the morning and by eleven o'clock the train had managed to crawl fifteen miles. The country, which at first was sand, soon became red granite. The view was monotonous though I did not find it unpleasant. A fine red dust was blowing in through the slatted window shades, giving our hands and our faces a dull tinge.

Around one o'clock the train stopped beside a pile of cut mulga stems in the middle of limitless plain. The engine driver and the fireman began leisurely to throw wood into the tender. We were glad of an excuse to get out and help. Sweat at once evaporated, though thin streaks of mud appeared on our faces. The country had changed; less vegetation and more dust appeared, and in a slight declivity an unexpected brightness, a river of white and pink blossoms. Here also last month's rain had brought forth flowers, the same kind of everlastings I had seen near Kalgoorlie, but smaller.

At two-thirty we reached a halt, a mere scatter of dusty huts with a huge water-tank raised on steel girders. One of the huts advertised itself as a coffee-palace; another displayed a drinking bar, where the population was gathered. We turned out to get what food we could, all of it from tins. Empty cans of many kinds formed the chief feature of this halting place, and scraggy goats were nibbling at the paper advertisements.

From here the train climbed slowly to the tableland of the interior. The air grew cooler. In places large areas were covered with white flowers; the earth had borrowed the lightness of the sky. The blown scent was wafted on the evening air.

At Yalgoo, which we reached at six-thirty, there was another halt. We got out to stretch our legs and find a meal. There had happened to arrive at just this time a team of sixty donkeys, drawing an enormous wagon laden with bales of wool from sheep stations further up-country. They were unspanned while we were at supper. About halfway through the meal, all the donkeys began braying at once. We went out to see. In a small decline behind the hotel, all sixty donkeys were rushing round, biting and kicking at one another, jumping on each others' backs.

"It's the time of day sets 'em off," one of the onlookers remarked, "just about twilight." Grey figures out of a twilight world, no mere fancies, but struggling hide and hoof, reeking of their own peculiar life.

Once again the train jerked forward, and as it jolted along the rails the screaming of the donkeys became distant. It was past midnight when we came to Mount Magnet, the junction for the Gascoyne branch; we were to go further to Sandstone which we did not reach before morning, after an uncomfortable night on hard wooden seats.

Sandstone, as I remember it, was not only red with desert dust, but most of the corrugated iron houses were painted a drab magenta. Only pepper trees were there; all other shrubs had been eaten by goats. In the hotel were the usual festoons of coloured paper hanging from the ceilings, thick in flies, dead and living.

At midday the atmosphere was so hot that one could not touch the metal of knives and forks. But at night the temperature fell quickly, and even in the hotel, where the warmth was held within the walls, I was glad of a blanket. We stayed several days, and here bought a cart and four horses. Outside the town there was a camp of natives who were more or less adapted to the presence of white Australians. Some of them could speak a broken pidgin English. I was filled with admiration to see how Brown got from them a great deal of the information he wanted. At first contact they began, one and all, to beg, but within a few minutes were offering anything they thought we might want: boomerangs, throwing sticks or spears. All of these Brown gently refused. Only later, and as a favour, did he accept one of their proffered gifts.

From the tribe that had made camp at Sandstone we persuaded two men to come with us as interpreters. This was against their natural interests, and it was entirely due to Brown's almost magical power over these people that they were persuaded. Their reluctance arose from their natural fear of going amongst strange and possibly hostile tribes. However, the prospect of sharing white-man's food tempted them. These bearded middle-aged men answered to the names of Tea-cup and Coffee; their native names were Mindooloo and Perrepierremarra.

There were rumours of tribal murders and two white men had been killed by tribesmen from the interior. They had abducted native girls without paying the demanded price. We subsequently found that even the wildest of the natives were easy to make friends with; we did not know this at the time, and had brought with us two watch dogs, a spaniel and an airedale.

After some days spent in preparation at Sandstone, we started for the interior. On our wagon were the tents, stores and the large tank of water for drinking purposes only. In this arid country there was little chance of a wash. We had our guns, rifles and bedding, and a large store of tobacco, pipes and beads as presents for the natives.

Water-holes are scarce in many parts of the bush, and the water which the natives find is frequently poisonous to white men on account of the strong salts. Lack of water is one of the hardships of bush life, and one misses a bath, feeling very sticky and dirty for the first few days. But after a while one gets accustomed to dirtiness, and hopes that a thick coating of dust may prevent bush-insects from biting so hard.

There were an enormous number of flies in the bush. They sat on one's clothes, making them black with their massed numbers, and it was difficult to eat or speak without a fly or two getting into one's mouth. Besides the little black flies that were so common, there were large yellow flesh flies, which the miners called bush humming-birds. These do not lay eggs but little wriggling maggots on food, clothes and blankets.

Within a hour of leaving the town we were completely swallowed up in the bush. Wherever we looked mulga and acacia bushes and stunted gum-trees grew from the bare red dust. The feathery branches seemed poised in the still hot air like hands lifted to command attention. For a great many years they had grown old and dry, brittle and thorny. The Western Australian bush gives the feeling of being very, very old indeed, and is now, as it was years before man was created, old and calm, with few sounds except the buzzing of flies and the whirring chirp of grey grass-hoppers.

There were few birds—an occasional rust-coloured crow, a few parakeets that screamed as their green wings flashed by, and sometimes flocks of tiny birds that swept from bush to bush with faint chirpings. The voices of the birds do not mingle as in Europe, but each one sounds separate and alone, emphasizing the stillness.

Among the larger animals in the bush, the ones that interested me most were the bandicoots. A bandicoot is rather like a ferret, but softer and more friendly; it will run away if one goes after it, but once caught it shows no sign of fear, and will readily take food from one's hand, eating with relish, sitting on its haunches, holding a grasshopper in small forepaws, nibbling and lapping up the green juices.

It is easy to catch bandicoots when one knows the way. The bandicoot makes a bolt for his hole and disappears. The hole is not deep and once its line is taken, it is easy to dig down and find the bandicoot crouched at the bottom. Its teeth are very small and can scarcely pierce a human skin, though they are well adapted to crunching insects.

During my time in the bush I kept several bandicoots as pets. As long as they were in boxes by themselves, all was well, but they would fight if confined two to a box. Although their teeth are small, their skins are easy to tear, even in handling. One bandicoot will kill another, and eat a large portion in a night. They are extremely pugnacious towards one another, but in other respects the most charming of the smaller marsupials.

Wallabies also were easily tamed and would stay with us so long as we fed them. They showed little fear of our spaniel dog, while

Australian natives beside a waterhole (*above*)
Aborigine man with throwing-stick and spear (*below*)

Bull-roarers and hair string made of human hair and wallaby hair

he survived before being eaten by the natives. He, poor creature, was so apprehensive of unseen dangers that he retreated if a wallaby showed a disposition to box. Kangaroos and wallabies box each other for fun, sparring in friendly fashion, keeping to regular rounds and resting between bouts; they are very playful, often stretching themselves in the most grotesque positions.

Among other animals in the bush, emus were common but shy, since the tribesmen were particularly fond of their innards; emu feathers were used for decorating head-dresses and for making shoes to disguise a man's footmarks when he was making magic. I persuaded our own tribesmen amongst whom we had our camp to spare one particular emu that I tried to tame. The emus are very inquisitive birds, and anything bright attracts them. I sat in the bush with a small mirror, and despite the continuous worrying of a multitude of flies, I kept as still as I could. After a bit my emu appeared. I flashed the mirror in the sunlight. At once it was obvious that he was interested. He came nearer. I continued to flash the mirror, and eventually he came to within a couple of yards of me, craning his neck, opening and shutting his large luminous eyes, and showing to good advantage his third lid. The time came when we looked each other squarely in the face, and I was not *quite* sure at that moment whether he was going to attack me. I stood up suddenly. He spread his plumy wings and dashed away at full speed. But this was not the last of our meetings; he often visited me again, and when I thought he was near enough, I would frighten him off. Before we left that district I gave him my mirror, which he received from my hand, and carried off with every sign of satisfaction. I hope he did not eat it.

The natives, with exceptionally good sight, are wonderful trackers. Once I was in the bush with a native, who was helping me in collecting insects, when I noticed an emu's footmark in the dust. I have prided myself on the keenness of my sight, and was stupid enough to point out to my companion the footmark, unwisely saying "emu". "Yes," he said, "and eight little ones." He did not actually say eight, but held up his fingers indicating the number.

This I thought was wonderful. Imagine looking at the mud in a chicken run, and saying how many chicken were there. This man had not only seen the little footmarks, which I had missed, but had seen that there were eight different pairs of baby emu footmarks. I thought the man was bluffing. "Follow up," I said, "see find 'em." He led me quickly at a half run, and in a short while we came on a father emu with eight little ones.

Emus, like ostriches, lay a large number of eggs at comparatively long intervals. The hen lays an egg every three days, and she lays from twenty to forty eggs. If she were to attempt to incubate them herself, those which were laid first would probably be addled before the later ones were laid. She does not, however, try to incubate all her own eggs, nor does she lay them all in the same nest. Two or three females associate together at the mating season, and place a large number of eggs in one nest; they also seem to lay very carelessly and drop a certain number of eggs haphazard. A male bird is associated with each group of females and he takes upon himself the task of incubation. Also he collects a number of the chance-laid eggs and brings them to the nest. He then sits upon the eggs and hatches them, and subsequently takes care of the young chicks. The hens, which have not yet laid their quota of eggs, then move on, leaving the cock to his task of incubation, and looking out for another cock; they will then make another nest, which will be taken charge of by a cock. In this way a fair proportion of the eggs are incubated while they are still fresh. This method of egg-laying and incubation shows an extraordinary adaptation to the realities of the situation, namely, the slow egg-laying propensities of the hens and the large number of eggs laid by each hen. The numbers of the sexes are approximately equal.

Another interesting animal which we saw in the bush was the bush-porcupine or echidna that lives most of its time in empty tree-stems that have been hollowed out by ants. I collected them in the same way that Gilbert collected rabbits, and had six of them tied to the pegs that held the guy-ropes of my tent. At night they were noisy companions, grunting and sniffing, straining at their tethers and scratching at the earth, but I managed to keep them all safely so long as I was in the bush, and during this time I learnt something of their habits.

In the daytime they remained under the sacks which I left for them. If the sacks were removed, they would press themselves close to the earth and tuck their long noses under their bodies, as though hiding their eyes from the light. In the evenings, provided all was quiet, they would walk to the limits of their tethers, and eat ants with their long extensile tongues.

The specimens which I kept in captivity for varying periods

from a week to a month were always shy and, unlike bandicoots, were not easily tamed. An observer must keep very quiet at a distance to see them in action. Sometimes I let them go free and followed them, and once had the good fortune to see one dig out an ants' nest and make a good meal. When my echidnas imagined themselves free and unobserved they moved at a fair pace, holding their bodies well up from the ground and flattening their quills upon their backs. None of my specimens had young during the short time they were with me, for I was too late for the breeding season. It is in September that the mother echidna lays her egg. The egg is soft-shelled, and it is probably laid directly into the pouch. The young is hatched in the pouch, where it suckles like any other young mammalian. During the time it is in the pouch it appears helpless and unprotected. Later, when it has grown its first few quills, it is deposited in a nest in some dry, safe place, where it remains till old enough to be weaned and able to look for ants for itself.

Australians who had captured these creatures when they were young told me that they could be tamed, coming when they were called and following their owners like dogs. My own echidnas remained wild and distrustful, and finally escaped in the hotel at Sandstone. I had hoped to keep them with me till my return to England. For safety I kept them in my bedroom, and since I was sorry to keep them constrained in sacks, I loosed them for the night, after locking the door to make sure they should not escape. As soon as the light was out they began marching round the room, pressing themselves between the wall and any piece of furniture, shoving everything about, and threatening to upset a heavy wardrobe. However, I did not think they could come to any harm, and I went to sleep.

In the morning I woke up to find every piece of furniture slightly out of place, and no echidnas. They had managed during the night to lift up a loose board in the floor, and had escaped under the hotel. There, unfortunately, I had to leave them, since the space between the flooring of the hotel and the earth was too small for me to crawl in after them. Both myself and the proprietor of the hotel were much annoyed at this unfortunate ending of my adventure with echidnas, but for different reasons. He thought they would disturb the other guests by shuffling and digging under the bedrooms, and I was sorry not to be able to keep them and observe their interesting breeding habits. One deduction I was able to make from this adventure: that these comparatively small animals were able to push about large pieces of furniture, using, no doubt, the strong digging muscles of their backs and shoulders.

In the bush near Sandstone we found only three species of snake: the black snake which was not uncommon, the death adder, and a small snake of mottled appearance of which I do not know the name. All were poisonous. We carried permanganate of potash crystals in case of a bite, but we never had occasion to use these. Snakes are usually timid animals and are more likely to be attacked by men than to attack.

Of lizards I found a large number of the species that were near neighbours to our camp. The most common were the little legless dust-lizards; these were eel-shaped, deeper than they were broad and well adapted to swimming in dust. They were difficult to catch and would try to bite, but were quite harmless.

Among the larger lizards there were the common bob-tailed lizards. These were about nine inches in length, slow in movement and easy to catch, but one had to exercise reasonable care, for they had strong jaws that could hold on as tight as a vice. The natives did not eat them, and I don't know of anything that did; I expect that was why they were so common. There were quick-running lizards that I could catch only with the aid of a horse-hair noose at the end of a stick. Slipping the noose over the head of the lizard was not always easy, as they were very much on the alert. With a rod with the hair-noose at one end in one hand, I would approach the lizard, at the same time making little patterns in the dust nearby with another stick in the other hand. The lizard would watch the moving stick, and while his attention was occupied, I would slowly approach with the noose and slip it over his head. Even when he was caught there was often a struggle, for a large lizard can bite hard and does not let go easily.

The largest lizards we saw were the big tree-climbing iguanas, which can be as much as five feet long. They have wonderful protective colouring and, when clinging close to a gum-tree branch, look like a thickening of the wood. The natives hunt them and eat them. I have tasted the flesh, and found it similar to a tough bit of skate. I once saw a native killing one of these. It died hard, and although it had a white-fellow's knife stuck through its head, pinning it to the ground, it wriggled and writhed, and contrived to hiss while its limbs and other portions were cut from it.

The smallest and most attractive lizards were the little geckos. These lived on, or under, the bark of trees. They have dull, protective colouring, and their eyes appear to be large and always open, because they have undeveloped eyelids. They have adhesive pads on their toes that enable them to climb vertical surfaces and to cling to the undersides of branches. They are comparatively slow-moving, and live almost entirely on insects; they approach slowly, stalking them, till at the last moment out flashes a long tongue, and the insect is seen no more.

The skint lizards, some of which were legless, lived in the all-pervading red dust. Some have transparent eyelids: they can shut their eyes to keep out the dust and still see through the transparent lids. The snake with its closed lids may well be a further development of adaptation.

As on the plains about Southern Cross there had been rainfall, so also in the Sandstone district; the desert flowers were not burnt up, and damp places remained where pools had formed. Natives dug for the toads that had buried themselves under the mud. It was surprising to think of toads living in such conditions, but toads there were. They have adapted by developing large sacs under the skin where they can store water. When the rainfall comes, they shuffle their way out, bathe in the shallow pools, mate, and lay eggs which quickly hatch into tadpoles. Then, pumping themselves full of water, they dig down into the mud again and thus survive. At times when water is scarce, the natives use some plants that have long roots or round roots like footballs, where water is stored. These can be squeezed; so also can the toads. We were often very thirsty but I was never driven so far as to squeeze a toad for a drink.

Most of the bush-frequenting animals are herbivores: the kangaroos, wallabies, boody rats, the larger lizards and, of course, the stick-insects, locusts and great grasshoppers. The bandicoots and some of the mice, the snakes, and most of the lizards are eaters of flesh; so too are many of the insects that prey, in one way or another, on the leaf-eating insects. The ants, of which there are great numbers, and many varieties, eat all they can find. Some ants are large and fierce. They will attack, and are extremely difficult to kill, even when crushed between two stones. The only way that we could deal with them was to burn out their nests, a hazardous undertaking, for desert ants can bite with one end and sting with the other.

The so-called honey-ants are comparatively innocent of fierce habits. They have a curious adaptation against the drought. Certain individuals are selected and confined to cells deep in the ground. During the time that the flowers flourish these ants are stuffed with honey by the workers to such an extent that their abdomens swell to the size of grapes. When the queens want food during dry spells these honey-ants are tickled under the chin, and they bring up their honey.

I have bought honey-ants from native girls. The living ant is held in the fingers and the abdomen bitten off. The taste is delicious, like honey with a slight formic-acid flavour. There are also large white caterpillars called bardi-grubs that live inside the stems of some of the larger bushes. The natives tickle them out with pieces of stiff grass. They are eaten raw, or put down beside the ashes of a fire where they swell like sausages and burst. I have eaten them reluctantly for I harbour a prejudice against caterpillars as food. They tasted too rich, I thought, like a mixture of marsh-mallow sweets and almond cream. Spiders of various sorts are also eaten with relish. Cockroaches, however, are left severely alone; their stench is warning enough.

The first night in the bush we neither heard nor saw any sign of the natives. On the second night we camped near a place where a big corroboree, or sacred dance, was to be held. Our two black boys told us that several tribes were meeting for the yearly celebration of dances connected with the coming-of-age of young boys; their own tribe was to be one of them. They lived near the station of a sheep-farmer, working at odd jobs on the farm and the women helping the farmer's wife with her washing. They seemed friendly enough, but were anxious for us to pitch our tents between their own tribesmen and a tribe from the eastern desert with whom they were at feud.

That night we saw nothing of these men; the country seemed empty save for ourselves and the friendly tribesmen, who squatted round their fires, chanting in a low monotonous sing-song, over and over again, words which sounded something like

"At my linga et un ja
Illa althara wantamar."

This they repeated over and over again, sometimes raising their voices, sometimes sinking them to a whisper. Now and then one of them would jump suddenly to his feet and shout, point into the bush, and say something rapidly to his companions. We could see no cause for these demonstrations, but noticed that our dogs appeared to be overcome with panic. Although we could see nothing for them to be afraid of, they trembled and slunk about with their tails between their legs. That night the airedale ran away into the bush, and we never saw him again. He was probably killed and cooked. The other took refuge, whining and shivering, in an empty packing-case.

After dark it was obvious that the country was not so deserted as it appeared. All round us we heard the sounding of bull-roarers. A bull-roarer is a primitive musical instrument. If properly swung it can make a very weird noise, which the natives believe is the voice of a great spirit; for them it has a sacred meaning. No man till he is fully initiated may see or handle one, and no woman is allowed to go near or see one. If she tried to do so she might be killed. This instrument, for them so awe-inspiring, is really very simple indeed. It consists of a piece of wood about eighteen inches long, three inches wide, and about half to three-quarters of an inch thick. It is flat, pointed at each end, and narrowed at the edges. At one end it is fastened to a long piece of string made of hair. To make the bull-roarer "sing", they swing it round their heads on the end of its string. As the wood flies through the air it vibrates, producing the strange intermittent sound. The vibration rises, and mutters, and sings, and very weird and wild three or four of these instruments can sound on a dark night in the bush. This was the first time I had heard them, though on later occasions I stood amongst the natives and swung a bull-roarer till my arm was tired, and blisters came on my hand.

From all directions the sounds came and we knew that many tribesmen were hidden in the darkness. Doubtless our dogs had been aware that large numbers of men were watching us. Our boys, Coffee and Tea-cup, were also frightened, and kept saying what bad, wicked men were the tribes from the eastern desert. For several days we remained in what appeared a slightly unsafe position between the native tribe we knew, and those who never showed themselves, though they made their presence known by bull-roarers at night and by the fear they inspired in our remaining watchdog.

We made contact with the wild tribesmen in an unexpected manner. I was walking with Brown some distance from our camp when we noticed sticks stuck upright in the ground. He suspected these marked some special territory, possibly a sacred place. In trying to avoid it, for we did not want in any way to outrage the feelings of the natives, we came on about twelve tribesmen seated on the ground in conclave. Brown told me to sit down. This was wise, for if we had gone forward, they might have been annoyed; if we had retreated, they might have thought we were afraid. At about a hundred yards distance they watched us until, after what seemed a long time, one of the men came over and began pouring out a stream of words, none of which we could understand. We remained seated until we guessed that he was inviting us to join his party. We then went over and sat down again, this time within the arc made by these wild fellows, who were quite naked except for a girdle made of bones and teeth.

While they continued to talk Brown followed his own technique, still remaining silent and looking intently, searchingly at each man in turn, demanding some sign of recognition and perhaps of friendship. In turn each man gave it, all except one who remained sulky and scowling. Brown was not to be put off, and it looked as though there was to be a conflict of wills until the other men convinced us that there was something abnormal about the sulky one. We found out later that he was deaf and dumb.

Brown now produced a magic stick that had been carved by some other tribe of aborigines. This produced immediate response, a repeated puffing sound—puff, puff, puff—and then a great many words. With a gesture for silence Brown began to talk slowly in English.

They did not understand his words any more than we understood theirs, but the fact of words exchanged made a bridge. Brown, wishing to include me in his new relationship, handed me the stick. Prompted by some deep unconscious motive of which I was not in the least aware, I made a loop between first finger and thumb of my left hand, and passed the stick slowly to and fro. This was met with roars of appreciative laughter and thus, by accident, we had established a human relationship more profound than any language.

Nevertheless, it was some days before all suspicion of us as white strangers was overcome. What really established our position was Brown's knowledge of the complicated marriage system of the Australian aborigines. Knowing the pattern from book-knowledge, he had the advantage, for they only knew it empirically. Gathering a few facts from them, Brown was able to deduce a great many other facts, and this was beyond their comprehension. It placed him in the position of a wise medicine man, or indeed higher, as one who had returned from the happy hunting grounds.

Each tribe is divided into two fratres, and each fratre into two classes—four classes in all. To avoid unfamiliar names, difficult to remember and differing in different tribes, I will call them A, B, C and D. A and B are of one fratre, C and D of another. Every man and woman knows from earliest childhood to which class he or she belongs. The system runs close to the following pattern, though there occur variations. An A class man will marry a C class woman. The children will go to the mother's fratre but to a different class from hers, namely D class. In like manner if members of B marry D, the children will go to the mother's side, but into another class. All possible marriages are known instinctively to every member of the tribe. Their knowledge consists of genealogies, extremely puzzling to an amateur anthropologist. I was constantly making mistakes, but Brown knew it all as well as the oldest and wisest of the elders. After asking a few simple questions the whole structure of the tribe was revealed to him and he knew who had conformed and who had erred, although these mis-marriages were far removed from the knowledge of the native who was questioned.

This power which we used to full extent was a kind of bluff, but it was extremely effective and secured us an assured position. We had carried, at first, heavy revolvers, but these we discarded for magic sticks concealed in small linen bags. The natives respected these, and would not pass by without some sign of recognition.

Coming from Europe where reason is supposed to rule, I thought lightly of magic, but not for long; for I have seen men die under magic spells, and have come to understand how life can be pervaded by magic, which for the primitive man combines both religion and science. He thinks or chants magic spells when chipping flint spear-heads or shaping boomerangs. Magic is related to his own body in so far as sexual responses are without direct volition, and every man's footmark can have a magical significance.

The lives of animals move also in a world of magic, and tribesmen trace their descent from animal ancestors. Kangaroos can on occasion be thought of as owning boomerangs, and snakes and bardi-grubs can be the makers of rain. Many of the stories and legends interpret natural phenomena in terms of the animal kingdom. The sun, for some tribes, is a burning emu's egg; others think of the sun as an old woman with a firestick wandering in search of her child. The moon is a man. At the new moon he is starving; he goes fishing, and as his endeavour is successful he grows bigger and bigger. Shooting stars are the souls of dead men dropping firesticks. The rainbow is a great fish swimming in the sky, drinking the rain. And the Milky Way is a great river full of fish.

One of the men who served us as handyman met his death by magic. One morning we noticed that he was looking very dejected. "What's the matter, Gnilgoto?" we asked.

"Me dead-fellow. Pointum bone, me dead-fellow."

To kill a man by magic is a fairly simple procedure. The evil magician retires to a remote spot; he places a hollow bone upright in the ground, and then for as many hours as he can sustain himself without food or water, he wishes evil into the bone. He curses every part of his enemy's body, then everything that he touches or eats, with the exception of water. When he has finished cursing, he starts all over again. And then again. When his bone is well loaded with bad wishes, he puts on a pair of shoes made of emu feathers. This is to prevent his footmarks being tracked. Then he leaves the bone where his enemy will find it.

Our boy had found such a bone. He had no idea who had made the magic. Unless he could find out and kill his enemy he would certainly die. And die he did, of a mixture of depression, fear and his own strong belief in the powers of ill-wishing.

Such are the powers of suggestion. But bush magic is not only suggestion. A man can be killed without knowing that magic has been made against him. When I first went into the bush I thought it was all nonsense and superstition, but by the time I had lived there a year, I was sure that great powers were hidden in magic and would on no account have risked having magic made against me.

During these early times that we spent with the natives we were hard at work making vocabularies. With the help of our native interpreters, we were making lists of what we considered essential words, some three hundred of them. These included attributes of the body, family relationships and, of course, the animals. From these vocabularies we could write down the equivalent native words, using Sweet's phonetics to help getting at unusual tones, such as *ng, th, pff, uff,* in many of the names. With these words we used English auxiliaries, and were able to communicate with the natives.

A few days after we had made contact, I had further proof of Brown's almost uncanny power. We were walking in the bush when we came on a number of men who, with shouts of defiance, were fitting spears to their throwing sticks, and vibrating them preparatory for the cast. Opposite them were men of another tribe in like position. Without hesitation, Brown's tall, imposing figure, in his white tropical suit, walked between them and, hardly raising his voice, ordered them in English to put down their spears. Incredible as it may seem, they obeyed. If a fight had been started it might easily have spread to the other tribesmen. His power over these simple-minded men was such that, in very fact, they considered him as returned from the dead. He had in a few days won their confidence through unfailing kindness, never using threat or show of force.

One of the most interesting events was the preparation of *waninga,* or head-dresses, to be worn at the corroboree. These were of mulga withies bent into various shapes, sometimes extended as much as four feet above the head. On the withies were tied or stuck feathers of birds and the pure white down of cockatoo. Low-pitched songs about birds and animal ancestors made a continuous crooning that endowed the tribe with renewed strength.

We were not sure which day the corroboree was to be, but were assured that we would be invited. It was just after midnight when I was awakened by a hand placed gently on my foot. When I had turned on my torch I saw the full-lipped faces of two aborigines, giving gestures for silence. Brown had been awakened at the same time, and as soon as we had slipped on singlets and dungarees we went with five other men. Quite a long way it seemed, and I remembered having been warned that one should never turn one's back on the untrustworthy natives. They were all around us and we were completely at their mercy. Never at any time did they show hostility and this was remarkable, for they and their kindred had in the past been horribly treated by white settlers.

At the appointed place we were met by the elders of several tribes. About the ground cleared for the dancers, spears were set upright, and from all directions came the whirring cadence of bull-roarers. Listening to that recurring, yet irregular rhythm that was as organic as any heart-beat, I felt myself lifted out of my present self into the strange and new, which was yet familiar. Away in the bush, hidden from sight, were aboriginal savages, standing with legs straddled, swinging the vibrating blades, summoning the ancestral spirits.

By the light of blazing firesticks, the principals who were to take part in the dance prepared for the display. Their bodies were oiled and blackened with soot, and on the black background white patterns, partly of clay and partly of cockatoo's down, were fastened by little drops of blood. Pricks were made, and where the blood beads gathered, the down was pressed; as the blood congealed, it stuck fast. In this way bright patterns were made. The *waninga* were circles into which the dancers pushed their faces. Only for short moments would they try them on, hastily putting them aside as though unwilling to let them be seen before the appointed time.

When all was ready we were led further through the bush to a large cleared space, where all plants had been removed and the ground beaten hard and smooth. Here several of the tribes gathered for the occasion were grouped, both men and women, about small fires into which they thrust their firesticks from time to time. As soon as we appeared a number of dogs of various sizes rushed at us, but these were driven off by the firesticks that were flourished in their faces. We were greeted by the other natives, and when all was quiet we sat down with our adopted tribe beside one of the small fires.

All this while the native songs had been rising and falling in accord with the whirr of the bull-roarers. It was extremely moving and I was caught away into the tribal collective, submerged in the pervading spirit of the bush. The nasal singing, the glowing circle of fires, stole from me familiar thoughts. I had the feeling that this had happened before, strange but somehow familiar. Something of the kind I experienced later in Fiji when drinking large portions of *yangona* had produced lulling of the accustomed senses and an awakening of new ones.

On one side of the stage was a high pile of brushwood. This was kindled and as soon as the flames got hold, a sooty and shining figure, wearing a *waninga*, came to the centre and began haranguing. All the women among the audience bowed their foreheads to the earth and began a wailing chant. Women might not see or hear anything pertaining to man-made religion, and for this reason they hid their eyes and filled their ears with their own wailing.

A few moments later eleven dancers, set in two rows, faced the audience. They were soot-blackened, with white patterns of clay up and down in stripes, blotches and rings; round their faces were *waninga*, and at knees and wrists tufts of feathers. These were animal ancestors, the *alchuringa*. In the light of the blazing wood-pile, they danced stiff formal dances, dramatizing mythological events. Their movements were deliberately unnatural, each gesture designed to convey an inward esoteric drama.

The dance lasted only a few minutes, for as soon as the flames subsided, the dancers withdrew, the herald again occupied the stage, the women looked up, ceased to wail, and began to laugh. The groups about the fires stirred, the bull-roarers ceased their droning, and the corroboree, for that night, was over. Dawn was breaking; the darkness had been vanquished. The performance for which long and elaborate preparations had been made was quickly at an end. For three weeks the natives had been preparing the ground, fashioning the *waninga*, and now in a few minutes the ceremony was completed; yet in that short time, the prehistoric had been brought into the present. The groups of the separate tribes had been welded into a single organism by the chthonic forces communicated to the dancers.

The natives have extraordinarily well-developed eyesight; they observe everything and have great ability to remember what they have seen. They can hear sounds that we miss and sometimes when I was looking for caterpillars or stick-insects, difficult to see on the dried mulga stems, I would get a native boy or girl to listen for the noise of tiny claws scraping on a leaf. But though they can see and hear so well, they are not so sensitive to pain as we are. They have rough games, one of which is to throw spears at each other's legs, warding off the thrown spear with narrow wooden shields. I have seen a spear go through the thick flank of a man's thigh; he laughed and broke off the end, then asked a friend to pull it out with his teeth. Their bodies are usually decorated with cuts and burns—long, deep marks on shoulders or across chests. They rub dust and ashes in the open wounds, so that they heal with thick rounded edges. Sometimes the girls wear a necklace of burns made by pressing a red-hot stick into the flesh; often they hold the hot stick themselves while it sizzles the flesh. Because they feel so little themselves, they are indifferent to the suffering of other living creatures; yet they are friendly and cheerful, and laugh a great deal.

They have only a few names for colours—yellow, red, white and black. They can count up to four; after four they speak of "many". They show hands and fingers up to ten, sometimes as far as twenty. They reckon a date by making marks on their bodies or on a stick, and every day removing one of the marks.

Their language is very complicated and extremely difficult to learn, far more so than ours; each tribe presents variants. Perhaps because their own language is so difficult they are very quick at picking up English.

In the early days of European colonization, there were large numbers of aborigines living in all parts of the country, in the fertile as well as in the desert parts; there were large tribes, but these are now shrunk to small numbers. The natives have died out before the advance of European civilization, and where there used to be hundreds of thousands there are now only a few thousands left, living in parts distant from the centres of civilization. The aborigines did not choose or prefer to live in the deserts; they survived there because the deserts were the last places to be explored by the white men.

One of the reasons for the inability of the two groups to live together is found in the brutal attacks that were made on the natives by the settlers. There is a place on the south coast where I have seen hundreds of skeletons of the aborigines who were slaughtered—men, women and children. The settlers came and took the best part of the land, where there was water and good food for cattle; they put up fences and turned loose cows and sheep. The natives had for many generations been accustomed to look on the land as their own; when they saw the cows and sheep grazing near their water-holes they could not resist the temptation of throwing spears at them, and no doubt they killed and feasted on a good many. They did not understand the white man's idea of keeping and breeding animals. Being hunters, not farmers, when they saw an animal their instinct was to kill it.

The killing of their stock made the farmers angry, and since they could not persuade the natives not to spear the cows, they banded together to hunt the natives and kill them. In some cases they hung up bags of poisoned flour. But neither poison nor rifle bullets was the chief cause of exterminating the earlier possessors of the land; it was rather the diseases brought by the white man. Whole countrysides were killed by measles and influenza. There were no hospitals or proper doctors, and so once they got ill, the natives died very quickly. When they saw their friends dying they became frightened and depressed, and as the white man spread over the land the natives lost their old tribal laws and customs which had kept them strong and self-reliant, and slowly lost their grip on life. Only in those parts where white men found life too difficult could they still survive, and even in the desert their numbers were much diminished. It was rare, at that time, to find a tribe with as many as a hundred individuals.

In each tribe the men, as hunters, killed the meat. The women with their digging-sticks dug for roots, collected edible fungi and found caterpillars and honey-ants. They did the work of the camp, and when the tribe trekked from one place to another, they carried the burdens. Each tribe had its own definite tract of country, its own dialect and social laws. Although the Australians wandered about from place to place, building no houses and merely heaping a few bushes together as shelter for the night, they kept to their own tract of land, never going outside it except when they were invited for inter-tribal gatherings and feasts. They were particular about this, and did not like trespassing on other men's ground.

The people, so long as they escaped the influence of the white settlers, remained true to their ancient ways. Their weapons date from the neolithic period. The spear-heads are well shaped, and made usually of chipped flint, but more recently of glass from white man's bottles. Sometimes I have seen a native squatting on his heels working patiently, often for several days on end, at the laborious manufacture of a stone axe. First he took a rounded stone of about the right size and roughly chipped it down with a piece of quartz to something like the desired shape; then with another smaller stone, he slowly and carefully chipped off small flakes until nothing of the original working was left. This process usually took two or three days. Next he rubbed the worked edges on a grindstone, using sand and water. These grindstones were of a special kind of rough sandstone; they were much valued, and were often carried for long distances by the women.

When the sides of the axe were quite smooth and a good edge had been ground, a tough flexible branch was twisted round the blunt part of the stone. The two ends of the branch were joined halfway down and bound by string or the tendons of animals. Lumps of resin were squeezed between the haft and the stone to hold it firm, the resin was smoothed by fire, and, last of all, the haft and head of the axe were coloured with red ochre. These stone axes were not often used in war, nor for killing animals; they were more tools than weapons, and were used for cutting notches in trees for footholds, or for splitting logs in which animals might be hiding, or trees where bees had nested. They were also used for shaping other weapons and for hollowing out wooden vessels.

For knives the natives used sharp pieces of flint or quartz, and, near the coast, sharp pieces of shell. Stone hammers were made without flaking and fitted into handles in the same way that axe-heads were fitted into their shafts.

The bones of animals were used for various purposes, sometimes as knives, but more often as sharpened awls for piercing skins. They were used too in connection with magic, but were most frequently seen strung together into necklaces. Strings of teeth were also made into necklaces and headbands.

The instruments manufactured by the natives were sometimes decorated with great skill. On their shields and bull-roarers they cut patterns and coloured them with pigments, usually yellow, white or red. They drew, with colours, elaborate patterns on their own bodies, and at sacred dances designed careful drawings on the ground, supposed to represent animals; but a white man, looking at them, would find them difficult to recognize. When we think of an emu we think of what it looks like, and when we draw it we draw its outline; the aborigine, though he may sometimes draw the outline, is more likely to represent what seems to him the most important thing about the emu, namely, its inside. His drawing of the emu is of two large lumps of fat, which lie on each side of the liver and are particularly good to eat. This drawing, which to a white man has no meaning, is understood at once by another native as being that of an emu.

One of the most important things that a native could make was string, which was made of the hair of animals mixed with human hair. Human hair, being longer than that of animals, had considerable value, and in some tribes there were curious systems of rights governing it. Usually there was a *tabu* between a man and his mother-in-law; that is, he was not allowed to look at her or speak to her, and must avoid her on all possible occasions. But in one tribe each man had rights over his mother-in-law's hair. When he wanted to make string, the law of the tribe decreed that she must cut off some of her hair for him.

In some parts of the bush, baskets were made by the men, but in the part we visited they used bags made of the skins of animals. These bags were usually fairly large, and the women carried in them a collection of odd things. First, and perhaps most important, was the baby that was sometimes to be found in it, but often there were many other things that must have been uncomfortable bedfellows. The explorer Grey found in an Australian woman's bag a flat stone to pound roots on, earth to mix with the pounded roots, quartz to make spears and knives, stones for hatchets, prepared cakes of gum for making and mending weapons, kangaroo sinews for sewing and binding spears, needles of kangaroo shin-bones, hair for belts, shavings of kangaroo skin for polishing spears, stone knives, red and yellow ochre, bark to carry water in, waist-bands and spare ornaments, pieces of quartz very precious and magical that had been extracted by medicine men from their patients, pieces of dry wood and fungus to make tinder, emu grease, roots collected during the day, and a baby.

Fire was of great importance to the aborigines. They carried fire about with them, never allowing it to go out but carefully tending it, transferring it from one dry branch to another. But for all their care fire sometimes must be kindled afresh. This is simpler to describe than to do. The man squatted on his heels (it was usually a man who made fire) and took two pieces of dry, soft wood, one about nine to twelve inches long, and the other flat and broad. The stick which had a blunt point at one end he pressed upon the other stick, and turned it nimbly by holding it between both hands, so that it turned quickly one way and then the other. While he did this he moved his hands up and down the stick, pressing down on the point as much as possible to increase the friction. In this way he could usually get fire in two minutes, but it was hard work. I have tried to make fire in this way, but in vain. I have known English boys who could chip flints as well as the aborigines, but never one who could make fire.

Although there is no education in the European sense of the word, the aborigines were by no means without a code of morals. Each boy and girl had to go through severe initiation ceremonies during which deep cuts were made and teeth knocked out. These ordeals were born with fortitude, for at each stage the boy or girl knew, after the ordeal, that he or she was now superior to those not yet initiated. The first initiation took place when a boy was about nine years old. He was made to fill his mouth with a large ball of string made of hair. This was to prevent his tooth being knocked down his throat. He was then made to lie on the ground and his potential wife's eldest tribal brother squatted above him and placed a wooden peg at the root of a lower incisor. The tooth was knocked out by a blow on the peg with a stone. After that everyone knew that the boy was so far initiated; the gap in his teeth remained all his life.

A little later he was taken into the bush by the tribal elders and shown the sacred caves and the sacred cave drawings, which, he was told, were made by animal ancestors. Later, near the end of his time of initiation, he was given a sacred name. The boys were circumcised with no better an instrument than a chip of flint. The girls had their hymens pierced with sharp sticks.

Until a young man had finished all his initiations, and there were seven of them, he was not allowed any physical intercourse with women or girls. The penalties were severe. And the laws were seldom or never broken for they had been literally cut or burned into the flesh of every man and woman. One of the men we knew told us this story.

Women, he said, have less respect for laws than men. When he himself had been through all the initiations but had not yet been told he might take a girl, he went hunting for honey in the bush. At the next corroboree in about a month's time he would be admitted to the rights of a full-grown man. He had caught a wild bee without letting it sting him, and was careful not to let it lose its sting, for if the bee stings it dies, and will not serve its purpose. On its back he put a small drop of his own blood, which acted as a sort of glue to attach a small bit of white cockatoo's down. Then he let go of the bee which set off, heavily laden, towards its home.

He could easily follow with his sharp eyes. He followed the bee to its nest in a hollow tree, climbed up and began breaking the wood with his stone adze. A girl who fancied him had followed him silently, and when she saw him in the tree, she threw a small stone that hit him on the leg. He looked down and saw the girl, and knew his danger, for like any other boy of his age he desired what was offered. He knew he must do something quickly if he was not to break the law. He jumped down, picked up his spear, and hurled it at the girl. It went deep into her breast, and she fell bleeding and crying out. He was frightened, for he was no natural murderer. He ran back to the tribe and told the elders what he had done, then took them back to the fatal tree. By the time they arrived the girl was dead.

A conclave was held, and the judgment was that he had done right. At the appropriate time he was given another girl as a reward for his pious action. As he told the story, he grinned and laughed. He knew he was a good and wise man. He had had several young wives since then.

After we had been collecting genealogies for some weeks, Brown discovered that there was a white man who had a cattle-station not far distant; he had lived in close association with the tribesmen for some years. We decided to visit this man, not only for the interest of meeting him but, since our water supply was low, in the hope of replenishing at some source nearer than Sandstone. With our native informant to guide us we set out, with cart and horse and our near-empty tank. After travelling some miles we came on a wire fence enclosing the wandering cattle herds of this remote rancher. Before long we saw his house, a sectional-built hut of jarrah wood. It had walls, doors and windows, but few other signs of its original structure. By shouts we tried to announce our arrival, but got no response other than the emergence from the hut of three aborigine women, all young and of comely proportions. Our guide, questioning them, found that the boss was away and would not be back before evening.

Looking in through the open door we could see the remnants of some mattresses that had been pulled to pieces and were now strewed on the bare wooden floor. Any other furniture that had once been in the room had been turned out into the yard. We pitched a small tent nearby, kindled a fire, and waited.

At dusk the white man returned. He was not the owner of the station but a paid manager. This we learned later; at first he was far from communicative. Indeed, he made it plain that our visit was unwelcome. We asked if we could take water from a rough well he had dug. He agreed, but hustled the black girls back into the hut, and himself turned his back.

All we could do was to fill our tank and then wait in the hope that his mood would alter. Brown instructed our own three natives that had come with us to mingle with the other natives that were camped about the station and to explain, if they could, the business that had brought us so far into the bush, and to make clear our neutral attitude. His idea was that the gossip would be communicated to the boss.

In this we were not disappointed, for after we had finished our evening meal and were sitting by our fire, the station boss came out and stood staring at us in a surly manner. Brown invited him to take a seat and offered some European cigarettes. After a short hesitation he accepted the invitation, and, seeing us in so fraternal association with our own natives, and hearing and understanding far more than we could of their lively communications, his attitude of hostility and suspicion relaxed. Had we any message for him, he asked. No, none at all, and Brown explained our mission.

He listened moodily as he smoked. A curious conversation followed partly in English, partly in native dialect. He told us that he was employed by a land-owning company, and that he was in charge of two thousand or so head of cattle. No complaints had come from headquarters, but rather commendation for the success of his management. He worked on a salary and a good one, but he had no use for money, seldom going so far as Sandstone, and then only to send in quarterly reports. He let us understand that he preferred the native way of life to that of Europeans.

Before long it was obvious that he was glad to talk with us. If only the whites would leave him alone, that was all he asked. The whites did not know how to treat the natives; as like as not they stole the young girls without paying the required sum in tobacco, or whatever. He had paid for his girls, and had found them far more accommodating than white women.

With a sudden gesture he bared his breast and shoulders, pulling down his shirt and exposing scars similar to those carried by the natives. "These scars show that I have chosen their way of life," he said. "I am one of them. I like this country, it suits me fine." Then he added, "When you go back do not talk about me. Let me be forgotten."

We stayed two nights and days with him. He told me that he had come to love these people, and had become a member of the tribe. "They have a religion," he said, "better than anything I have found amongst white men." He showed us with pride the coffee-coloured children that squatted among the ruins of his one-time mattresses. "They will be better off here than in Perth. My accounts are straight. There is nothing to complain of. These men work for me for nothing. What more can the owners want?"

We liked him, and I think he liked us. He had assimilated his environment, yet despite his affirmations, there were indications that he was not quite at peace with himself. We wondered how long the simplicity and adaptability of the native girls would satisfy the restless ego of a European. However, his anecdotes, together with the story told by the pious aboriginal youth, who, rather than yield to the over-bold approach of a young woman, would risk her death and his own, helped make a picture in our minds of the integration of an aboriginal tribe.

We returned to our headquarters with a full water tank, feeling well rewarded for our journey. However, it was not long before misfortune came upon us.

I was awakened one morning at the earliest streak of dawn by the barking of dogs, the screams of native women and the sound of revolver shots. I jumped up, pulled on my dungarees, and dashed out to find Brown standing outside his tent, the flap of which was down. The police from Sandstone, aided by some local young men, were riding through the camp, firing off revolvers at the native dogs. The natives in confusion were making themselves scarce among the mulga bushes, and in a short while all the aborigines together with the horsemen had disappeared.

Brown was in a silent angry mood and when the chief police officer returned a few minutes later, he was at no pains to be polite. He listened to the man's story about dangerous murderers; they were tribal murders, but still murders, and his headquarters had told him to make arrests. Brown asked whether they had caught any of the dangerous men. Yes, they had one, but the policeman was not sure they had the man they were looking for. With some bitterness Brown told him that the raid had ruined nearly ten weeks of work. While their talk was going on an ancient native was brought in, his arms twisted behind his back by his captors. He did not look like a murderer, and protested that he was not, but after some altercation he was carried off to be put in jail in Sandstone.

When the police and their young men had departed and we were alone in the empty bush, Brown lifted the flap of his tent, and there emerged two of the supposed murderers who had taken refuge with their white-man friend. We gave them some food to comfort them, and they departed to find their tribesmen. A tribal murder is not really a murder in malice, but a natural killing to compensate for supposed magic-making. If a man dies for no apparent reason, it is assumed that magic has been made against him. His body is put in a tree, and when some fat has run out of it, the fat is caught on dried leaves and the leaves kindled. The bad magic comes from the direction that the smoke is wafted. His tribal brothers set out, and spear the first man they meet. This is an established custom.

Despite their trust in Brown the natives did not return; only one of them did, and he was the white-haired old gentleman who had been carried off by the police. The next morning we found him stark naked sitting beside the embers of our camp fire holding a glowing stick to various portions of his body, hoping in this way to warm his shivering person. He explained that his captors could find no charge against him, and had let him go. He had run all the way from Sandstone during a day and the following night.

This unfortunate incident completely changed our plans. It was obviously impossible to follow the dispersed tribesmen, and so, after waiting for a few days to see if any would return, Brown decided to go to the islands in Shark's Bay where there were natives collected in lock hospitals. We packed our tents and returned to Sandstone. There we sold our horses and the cart, and returned on the antediluvian train to Geraldton.

My first plunge into the clear, warm, beautiful sea at Geraldton I shall never forget. The caked dust of ten weeks was washed off and I knew again the joy of being clean. From Geraldton we had a rough journey on a small coasting steamer to Carnarvon, the port for the islands. The steamer was very small, about two hundred tons; she rolled and pitched and I was dreadfully seasick. How glad I was to be on firm land again and getting into the truck of a still more primitive train than those already experienced. This took us across Babbage Island and over a causeway to the mainland and the town of Carnarvon.

THREE

Shark's Bay

H ERE AT CARNARVON, which was at that time a desolate
cluster of iron-roofed bungalows set in a yet more desolate landscape, we began to ask about getting over to the
islands. We were recommended to an old seaman named Henrietta.
He was in charge of the ten-ton cutter the *Shark*, a government-
owned boat, once a good vessel but now in decline. Henrietta was
the very likeness of a Daddy Neptune, of large girth, ample beard,
blue watery eyes and possessed of most enormous feet, which,
through having been exposed for so long to salt water and tropical
sunshine, were two or three times as large as feet normally are.
He was a "wet bob" if ever there was one, genial and good-
tempered, and not to be hurried. He drank deeply and often, and
on many occasions was sunk in drunken sleep from which nothing
could waken him. He was assisted in his island-journeyings by a
small sailor boy called Toby, a great fisherman who invariably
cooked the fish he caught in plain sea-water, serving them, scales
and all, without any accessories.

After many delays, we loaded our stuff on board, bags and bags
of it, for we went provisioned for several months. The journey
was a delight: the blue, sparkling, tropic sea, the stiffening breeze,
the sense of adventure, the plunge into the unknown. Other
details of the voyage were the sight of acres—yes, literally acres—
of sharks' fins cleaving the sea's surface as the sharks lay basking,
and the sudden appearance close to our craft of huge turtles, who
lifted their shell-and-weed-encrusted carapaces out of the
transparent waters and, with enormous sighs, greeted us, sinking

again with gurglings and upbubblings into the depths. And there was Henrietta. He knew all the coast from Carnarvon to Wyndham, and talked with a rare, salt flavour to his words, chuckling at his own stories, as his great feet splayed the deck and were themselves wonders of biological interest. He was glad enough to let us sail the boat while he sat in the shade of the cockpit and let drop, as occasion offered, his wisdom.

Although the wind was blowing half a gale at noon, and we had been forced to reef, it declined with the sun; we were not in time to avail ourselves of the land breeze to make the bay close to the hospital, but had to row in the dinghy through the quick-failing light to a small cove at the southeast of the island. Brown, a rouse-about, called Louis, whom we engaged to help with the work of the camp, and myself with a new dog were got ashore together with our camp-beds and other essentials. On Henrietta's advice we camped on the sand to avoid the ants, which he said were "terrible bad" inland. We made a fire of dried seaweed and flotsam, and cooked our supper in the dark, while all around us swarmed multitudes of quick-running crabs which scuttled in long, echelon formations, lifting their stalked eyes like periscopes and flapping them back into their appropriate grooves at any alarm. That night we slept with the stars above, crabs underneath, the unknown island on one side, and the sea's wavelets lisping up the beach on the other.

The next morning we made up the coast to the landing-bay. Here we disembarked all our gear, helped by the resident stockman, whose official duty was to look after the few sheep and cattle on the island, but whose real function was to keep order amongst the native patients. This he did roughly, but not with undue brutality. Indeed, he was sorry for them, and ran considerable risk of infection on their behalf.

We established camp about half a mile from the hospital, and our first task was to deal with the ants. We dug out their nests and filled them with hot ashes. This kept them occupied for a while. As soon as they had things a bit straight, and were again on the prowl, we gave them more hot ashes. Our war was never completely won, but we kept them in check. Most of our time on the islands, we had to hang up our boots and clothes on the tent poles to prevent them being eaten during the night. Even our toe-nails were attacked while we slept.

Life on the islands, despite ants, centipedes and small scorpions, and a great number of ticks, was far pleasanter than life in the bush. Here on the edge of the sea a breeze freshened up soon after sunrise, increased in strength with the day until noon, when it was blowing half a gale, then sank as evening approached to a dead calm after sunset. The flies were blown clear of us during the daytime hours, and this was a great blessing. We worked under a large awning; here we interrogated the natives, and when we needed refreshment, the sea stretched its clear blue water invitingly for us to bathe. At first we were a bit shy of the sharks, of which there were an infinite number. They were well fed on the huge shoals of fish. Dr. Hicksey, who was in charge of the hospital, was bolder than we, and would swim far out to sea. He was never attacked. He claimed that the sharks were timid creatures who would turn away if he splashed his cupped hand on the water.

Bernier Island was about eighteen miles long, and never much wider than a mile across, often considerably less. It was un-inhabited except for the hospital occupants and consisted of a central ridge of decaying coralline rock, and sand dunes on each side. To the west, the Indian Ocean sent its great rollers smashing on a wide shelf of submerged reef. On the eastern shore were a number of sandy bays where clear and azure waves broke gently and where vast shoals of sharks basked in the hot, bright sunlight or in the evenings came close inshore to scratch their bellies on the sands. Here were sheltered beaches of yellow sand, where the running crabs marched to and fro in armies, popping in and out of their holes and flicking their eyes up and down. These were often amusingly, though tiresomely, inquisitive. If one sat on the beach to rest or merely to enjoy sun and sea, they would poke with pincers hoping for something edible.

The days and weeks passed to the rhythm of good health and hot sunshine. At midday our shade temperature usually recorded a hundred and fifteen, but the dry wind made even this great heat endurable. By sunset it was cool enough to need a sweater. It seemed a perfect climate.

The vegetation on Bernier was adapted to a low rainfall: stunted acacias, banksias and grevilleas, and on the sand dunes mesembryanthemum and wire-like grasses, and, in places, some salt-bush. There was great diversity of animal life, untouched as yet by civilization. The largest mammals that inhabited the low-growing, prickly scrub were banded-wallabies, which abounded in great numbers. These were nocturnal in most of their activities, although they might frequently be seen in the day, leaping in and out of the scrub with the characteristic kangaroo jump. At night they would come fearlessly into our tents and scamper about, playing their games under our camp beds.

I was puzzled to know what these wallabies drank. There were no streams or pools of any kind on the island, and rain was a rare occurrence. I was surprised to learn they drank sea-water. I have watched them go along their regular runways at twilight to the edge of the beach; after a short hesitation they crossed the sands to the waves, and there quenched their thirst. Not only wallabies drink sea-water, but so do marsupial mice, of which there are two or three species indigenous to the island. These drink from salt-water pools and puddles. They have become adapted to the arid conditions of the island; it is probable that they lick up some drops of dew from time to time, but for their chief supply of liquid they must go to the sea. They have learnt how to tolerate and deal with the high percentage of salt that they must swallow.

Mosquitoes had also adapted themselves to the absence of fresh water; they bred in the rock pools, as they do in England and elsewhere. Whether the lizards and snakes of Bernier Island, of which there are large numbers, drank the sea-water, I do not know; I have never seen either snake or lizard do so. Perhaps, like the majority of insects, they get their moisture from the food they eat.

Many of the snakes and lizards are adapted to living in sand, through which they can wriggle as an eel does through water. Some species of lizards, to make this process easier, are legless like slow-worms, but far more agile. At the approach of a footfall they disappear in the sand in a way that reminds one of the quick back-flash of some of the sea-worms. Most are swift-running or swift-diving, though one of the most conspicuous of the island lizards is the slow-moving stump-tailed lizard, who cannot hurry his deliberate pace.

The lizards and snakes on Bernier Island were much infested with ticks. These were usually attached to such places where they could not be rubbed off. Ticks are never easy to remove, and on snakes or lizards, bedded between scales, they have a particularly firm grip. Ticks also infest wallabies, and will readily bite humans. They are insignificantly small when they make their landing on the host, consisting merely of a shrunken thorax and eight little waving legs. At the end of a night's feed, their abdomens are swollen to the size of grapes, and they are an alarming sight when discovered in a line, marking the place where a belt has pressed about the waist. They are difficult to remove; they burst easily, and their heads, unless properly pulled out, will become the origin of sores which take long to heal. There were millions of ticks on Bernier Island, the great majority of which lurked in the dry seaweed that fringed the beaches. Why they should be there, or what they could expect there, I could never guess, but I soon learnt to avoid the heaps of dried kelp that lay between the sand dunes and the beach.

Vast numbers of insects, spiders and millipedes inhabited this small island world. The centipedes and the scorpions had a dangerous sting, and one of the spiders, a black one with a red spot on his tail, could give an equally unpleasant bite. The most noticeable of the butterflies was an insect a little larger than our British large white, and of the same tribe, pale yellow and black on the upper surface and on the underside white, orange-red and black in a most handsome pattern. The bright colours were no doubt a warning that it was not pleasant to eat. These were very common and fluttered in gay flocks, care-free and confident, over the thorny bushes. A smaller yellow butterfly, which I took to be of the heath tribe, was of a delicate yellow with chocolate trimmings. This was almost equally common, and, of course, there were many other species. All were beautiful, both when seen in their wind-swept flocks, and individually, when scrutinized at close quarters through a lens. I could not help wondering, though the question may seem foolish, why they were so beautiful. Had they any aesthetic appreciation of each other's beauty? I could hardly think so.

Among the sand dunes, if I could endure the heat, I could always find the busy, self-absorbed microcosm of insect life. Most noticeable were the ant-lions, which pitted the ground with their miniature cone-shaped traps. Down at the base, if one paused to look, one might see the strong mandibles of the hidden insect thrust forward in anticipation of any ant or wandering creature that should slither down the incline. They did not have to wait long, and many victims I have seen pulled under to be devoured. Large numbers of ichneumon burrowed tunnels in which to store semi-paralysed spiders or caterpillars. These predacious insects expressed by their ecstatic movements the delighted satisfaction with the best of all possible worlds. They

were adapted to perfect harmony. All that they desired was
theirs. Very different was the expression of the heavy, herbivor-
ous profile of the long-antennaed locusts. These when free and
unmolested had always a somewhat harassed look. When paralysed
by a poisonous sting, and dragged on their backs by some
ruthless hymenopteron, they were as sheep brought to the
slaughter.

There were miniature bees and wasps that burrowed and
brought forth their tribes in the firmer, harder sand. There were
thineads and hover-flies and innumerable species of diptera. All
had their place, and contributed to the predestined pattern of
shifting sand and sun-glare.

Ants were forever running hither and thither, some very small,
some an inch long, which were impossible to crush. They were
immensely muscular and could carry burdens twenty times their
own size; sometimes they progressed backwards over the slipping
sand, dragging caterpillars, beetles or butterflies. Many of these
struggling pillagers fell into the traps of ant-lions. They disappeared, and it seemed they had never been.

At last, scorched by the blazing heat, I would leave the dunes,
gladly facing the breeze as I went down towards the waves.

The frontier between land and sea, always so rich with life, is
in the tropics a source of delight and discovery to any naturalist.
At night the sea turtles come up to lay their eggs, a clutch of from
eighty to a hundred buried in the sand and there left to hatch.
When the little turtles come out, they have to make a dangerous
journey back to the waves. They are soft-shelled, helpless, and
doubtless succulent. Sea birds in flocks attack the infant wanderers.
and those that reach the waves meet still other enemies. Fishes of
several kinds swim close inshore to devour them, and all that the
little turtles can do is to go steadily on towards the deeper water;
then, at best, they are alone with their bare lives in the great
unknown ocean. Slowly their carapaces harden, and, as they grow,
life becomes less dangerous.

Wherever rocks jut out among the sands, or cliffs come down
to enclose the bays, limpets, chitons, barnacles, and all such
sedentary tribes are gathered in their thousands. Of most
practical interest to hungry men are the small but sweet oysters
which, clustered upon themselves, make rocks of their own
groupings. Individually they are brittle and hard to open, and I
have found that the best way of getting at their interiors is to

break off a lump from the main colony and place it close to a
fire. Soon the mouths gape open, and the sweet contents can be
eaten. I found them much nicer than the European species.

On the west coast there were no sandy beaches, only piles of
pumice stone against the cliff foot. Between the cliff and the sea
at low tide was a shelf, a hundred yards wide or more, of denuded
coral, divided by numberless channels and rivulets and pitted
with rock pools. Often I would spend the hours between the tides
going from pool to pool, collecting specimens or catching the
crayfish or the large prawns that abounded there. The pools were
of all sizes, some large with sandy bottoms, excellent for bathing,
but most of them small and rocky, all brimming with clear warm
water, constantly refreshed by the swirl of waves that, breaking
on the outer edge of the reef, sent their waters landward. Each
pool was a tropical aquarium with delicate, brilliant corals, and
even more brilliant minute tropical fish lurking amidst the
coloured fronds of madreporite and algae. Anemones, echinoderms, holothurians, crabs of many kinds, sea slugs, sea mice,
and countless other creatures were here in abundance, either on
the rock faces or in the weed, and round the edges of these
miniature watery worlds were to be seen at night thousands of
small phosphorescent medusae with down-hanging tentacles.

Time slipped away unperceived on that coral shelf between the
land and the sea. Although for the most part engrossed, I would
sometimes, on looking up, see the great rollers of the Indian
Ocean banked high against the western sky, and it would seem
that they must, from their high altitude, sweep me away. But on
the unseen ledge of rock they broke, crumbled and dispersed, and
their waters, tamed by the impact, came harmlessly swirling
landward to ripple round my knees.

The scene on the eastern coast was altogether different. Here
there was nearly always a sense of calm and serenity, and this
calmness was more particularly manifest where the cliffs fell
steeply into deep water. Sheltered by the land, I anchored in a
small boat to fish, or to gaze down through a glass-bottomed
bucket into the clear depths. Many shoals of fishes passed like
shadows, and on one occasion, close inshore, I had the good
fortune to get fairly close to some dugong that were feeding on
tufts of seaweed. Waving their fore-flippers in an underwater
dance, they glided along the cliff foot as they munched the weed.
At what seemed long intervals they rose to the surface for breath.

Making deep exhalations, they thrust up their bewhiskered muzzles and gazed wonderingly around.

Much of our food came from the sea. Snapper were the best and commonest eating-fish. They would bite most readily just after the turn of the low tide; then we could pull them in, one after another, as quickly as we could cast our lines. The average snapper in Shark's Bay was from ten to twelve pounds, but from this weight only three pounds of filleted flesh could be cut off; the rest was head and bone. One of the most lovely fishes in the southern seas, its colours were a blend of purple, pink, orange, green and grey. Flat-fish of various kinds could be caught with bottom-bait. Stingarees were only too numerous and dangerous, for should one tread barefoot on the dorsal spine, the wound is dreadfully painful. I have seen aboriginal natives, who are singularly insensitive to pain, convulsed in agony from a stingaree wound. The spine at the root of the tail is covered with mucous skin, and this is poisonous. However its effect can be almost instantaneously neutralized by an injection of permanganate of potash. Stingarees, which in Shark's Bay can measure five feet across, can be harpooned and dragged ashore, an exciting sport which is much appreciated by the natives. When the fish is fighting in the surf, a man armed with a short stick will run as close as he dares and seize the long tail. As soon as he can get a bite on the tail with his teeth, he places the stick—holding it at each end—between the spine and the tail. With a downward jerk he can break off the spine, and then the stingaree is no longer dangerous.

These big flat-fish, the stingarees and skates, and also several of the sharks, live for the most part on molluscs, whose shells they break and grind up between their powerful and flattened teeth. There is competition between the hardness of the mollusc shell and the power of the fish to break it. Some of the cowries are very hard, and so too are the enormous clam-shells, which are unbreakable in their later stages of growth. They are vulnerable, however, to a small worm which burrows through the shell and reaches the tender interior. Thus the undersea balance of competing life retains equilibrium.

Of the birds that frequented the littoral, the pure white terns were the most numerous. They laid eggs just above the line of kelp, and reared their broods of young, apparently unmolested by the ticks that swarmed there. A large black oyster-catcher was common, and there were several kinds of gulls, whose names I did not know. A white eagle was the largest sea bird of that coast. The young of the first and second year were of mottled brown plumage. They grow increasingly white as their years advance. Some authorities say that they are pure white by their tenth year, others that they take twice that time to reach maturity. They were about the size of the British golden eagle, and, although these islands had only recently been inhabited by a gun-firing man, they were remarkably shy. They nested on the cliffs in inaccessible places. They dived like peregrines, with wings folded, and seldom failed to secure their fish. They did not penetrate the water as deeply as gannets, but only touched the surface and rose quickly from the splash.

On this island where no conventions need be observed, and where indeed many of the bonds of European civilization soon become loosed, I spent four happy months, during which time I felt myself grow closer to nature than I had ever been in England. I taught my skin how to resist the burning sun, and was soon able to go about with only a folded towel about my waist and a pith helmet on my head. I learnt to know and appreciate the touch of the warm sun-soaked winds. A new sense developed, a rich experience that can only be had by men who live in warm climates. Clothes not only limit our appreciation of the world, they cut off whole ranges of sensations which, when developed, convey an awareness of the pervading serenity of which even civilized man can learn to be a part.

The lock hospital on Bernier Island had been inaugurated by the Australian government with most admirable intentions. The problem of syphilitics and otherwise venereally-infected natives could no longer be altogether ignored. White men had brought these diseases to a race who had little or no resistance to infections which were at that time unknown to them. Syphilis, in particular, assumed surprising and dreadful forms, and in the nature of things the diseases spread and came back to the white settlers with gathered potency. The idea was to collect all infected cases and isolate the men on Bernier Island and the women on Dorre Island, both of which lay some thirty miles from the mainland in Shark's Bay. Hospitals were built and a doctor appointed in charge of both islands. He had to travel in a small sailing boat from one to the other.

The method of collecting patients was neither humane nor scientific. A man, unqualified except by ruthlessness and daring and helped by one or two kindred spirits, toured the countryside, raided native camps, and by brute force "examined" the natives. Any that were obviously diseased or were suspected of disease were seized upon. Their hands, which were so small that they could slip through any handcuffs, did not offer sufficient means of control, so their necks were chained together. They were marched through the bush in further search for syphilitics. When a sufficient number had been collected, the prisoners were marched to the coast, and there embarked on an ancient lugger to make the last stage of their sad journey. These journeys, from start to finish, often took weeks, and many prisoners died by the way. Flies in clouds buzzed about suppurating sores. The chains were never removed, for if they had been the natives would have been quick to escape. Men and women were mingled, and it was not surprising that all the survivors were thoroughly infected by a variety of ailments by the time they arrived at their destination.

On the morning after our arrival we were visited by the doctor who seemed pleased to see us, and we made the acquaintance of the stockman who took charge when the doctor was absent on his visits to Dorre Island.

My tasks in helping Brown to make and check genealogies were congenial, and apart from this work I was free to collect specimens of all the fascinatingly new creatures that inhabited the island and nearby ocean. Days and weeks passed for us in our camp in a kind of paradisaical calm, though they were by no means so calm for the occupants of the hospitals. After a while, however, our stores came near to an end despite the abundance of food that we caught in the sea: we needed flour, vegetables and tinned food, and it was decided that I should return with Henrietta next time he came over with our mail. For the first time I was to be in charge of our affairs with a sufficient amount of money to buy what I thought fit. I should have control of the boat most of the way, for Henrietta was always willing to let me sail while he sat in the little smelly cabin smoking his pipe, and Toby fished with spoon-bait over the side.

With a fresh wind we went too fast for spoon-bait fishing, but when the wind was light an occasional fish was hooked. All this I found very pleasant. The distance as a bee flies was about thirty miles, but with tacking and allowing for drift the journey was sometimes nearly sixty. It could, with good luck, be accomplished in a day.

The voyage I found full of incidents. There were flying-fish and flying-gurneys that chased them; there were Portuguese men-of-war floating and sailing by. Best of all was the sea breeze, and the wondrous scents of the ocean itself.

When we arrived at the long pier that was at the end of the light rail that ran across Babbage Island to the mainland, it was late evening. Henrietta and Toby said they would go along to the hotel, but having had some experience of upcountry hotels in the northwest, I decided I would sleep on deck. *The Shark* was made fast to some moorings, and I settled down on the hard planks of the deck with a blanket under my head for a pillow. Here on board I was clear of all mosquitoes, and I was well accustomed to hard beds. Indeed I thoroughly enjoyed it, most of all the solitude, and as I lay there I watched the mast-head trace patterns among the stars as the light faded.

The sound of soft lappings of wavelets on the sides of the boat was just the right sort of companionship that a desire for solitude could ask. I slept soundly and woke with the dawn. I had a dive overboard, but did not dare swim far, for I was still afraid of sharks. Then I waited till the first trucks with their small engines came out to the pier-head, pulling the bales of wool that were to be shipped south on the Singapore–Fremantle boat.

Carnarvon I found to resemble Geraldton in many respects, but the hinterland seemed considerably more barren. The town was full of men from the surrounding district, for the annual horse races were in full swing. I had not much time for these. My business was to buy stores, and return as soon as possible. The buying of the stores was not difficult, but once Henrietta was ashore and comfortably settled in the bar of a hotel drinking with his pals, it was hard to move him. As the days passed he became more and more inebriated, and I was at my wits' end how to get him to move. I had not the authority to sail without him. I was a mere Johnnie of an Englishman, and little more than a boy in the eyes of the Australians. There were plenty of excuses why we should not go, and I saw that I must wait till the races were ended. I returned to collecting of creatures, and Babbage Island was the obvious place.

Babbage Island was about three miles across, a wild barren spot lying in the shallow water of Carnarvon Bay. To the pier at the end of the railway came the coastal steamers; the arrival of each boat was an event not to be missed by the dwellers in an isolated township. Those who could spare the time crowded on to the trucks to go and meet the ships, and view the varied human specimens that composed their crews. Here could be bought bananas, mangosteens, mangoes, oranges and lemons; trades of many kinds were afoot, drug and pearl smuggling not excluded.

On a clear, cool evening I made one of the party going to visit the Singapore boat. The dusk came quickly, and as I had no friends or acquaintances on board, I climbed to the top of the high pile of bales that were there waiting to be embarked, after the initial business of unloading had been accomplished. I was alone on the top of the bales at about mast height, and could easily survey the whole length of the brilliantly lit ship. She had not only her ordinary illuminations but huge arc-lights, which were giving out a whitish-blue glare for the unloading of the holds. Almost naked Chinese coolies were at work, their sweat-drenched bodies gleaming like the scales of fish newly pulled from a phosphorescent sea. In the stern a cod-faced Chinaman was dangling a line overboard. He was motionless, without expression, seeming quite cut off from all the activity around. Along the passages and companion ways coffee-coloured stewards hurried with drinks on trays, and white men and women surged to and fro, in and out of the deck cabins. The boat hummed with the diverse noises of humanity, and I, from my vantage point on the wool-bales, watched and took in some portion of that life, and felt it mine; yet I was aloof from it, though tasting with appreciation its mixed savours.

For some undiscovered reason the moments burned with an extraordinary brilliance, and looking back over the long years between, that tropical night-scene appears one of those rare events when life's rising wave breaks in foam. I felt exalted, beyond myself. Like Whitman, I felt myself to be one and identical with the existence of other individual men, and I could not be troubled to move out of that aura of wonder where I then dwelt. I decided to let the train go, and to walk back at my leisure along the three miles of embankment across Babbage Island to the mainland.

I watched the swarming gangways, saw the people crowd into the trucks, and when at last the train had steamed out into the darkness, I lay back and looked at the stars.

This sight strangely contradicted, yet complemented, the other, and complemented also, in a full and satisfying manner, something within myself. For a long while I stayed there, and must have dozed, for when I awoke the activities of the ship were much subsided. The arc-lamps were no longer burning, the hatches were covered by tarpaulins, and most of the ship's company were between decks. Only the cod-faced Chinaman did not seem to have moved. He was beside his line, with his gaze fixed on the drifting float, just as he had been before.

I clambered down and began my journey back along the embankment towards the town.

Babbage Island is a low-lying bit of sandy land, and quite flat. The railway is raised some ten feet or so above the surrounding level for most, if not all, of the way. Along the side of the rail runs a narrow path, and along this I walked. My serene mood stayed with me, until suddenly I became aware of threatening grunts which drew quickly nearer. Looking round, I was horrified to see a large bull camel mounting the slope of the embankment, and making in my direction. His intentions were obviously far from friendly. In a flash I realized that I was in deadly danger, for what was to prevent this cross-tempered brute from overtaking me and chewing me to pieces? Such things had happened, and the semi-wild camels, when encountered on foot, were to be feared.

I ran as fast as I could, but the camel ran too, and I could hear that he was gaining. If I went along the path he was sure to catch me. I sloped down the embankment, and ran along in the shadow. The camel followed close, and in a few more steps would have caught me had I not chanced on one of the low tunnels, about five feet high, that had been made under the embankment to allow water to flow through at times of exceptionally high tide. Into this I dived, and there, gasping for breath and very thoroughly frightened, I crouched down, hoping the camel would miss me in the darkness, as at first he did. Soon, however, he returned and recommenced his grunting and snorting at the mouth of the tunnel, which was fortunately too low for him to enter.

We had reached an impasse: the camel could not get at me so long as I was in the tunnel, as he was too tall to enter, but on the other hand, I could not stay there indefinitely. No one would miss me at the hotel, no one would come to look for me.

I began to remember that I had seen these short tunnels traversing the embankment at more than one place. Probably they were at regular intervals. I would have to make a bolt for it, and so when I had made sure that the camel was at the right-hand entrance, I slipped out at the left, and ran as fast as I could under the protection of the embankment. The going was uneven and the way impeded with scrub, and in order that I might get on faster, I ventured up on to the path again. This may or may not have been a mistake, but anyway the camel got sight or sound of me, and took up the chase.

Again I dived into a protecting archway, and recovered breath, and now gradually my sensations changed. I was not so frightened as I had been at first; I felt I was playing a more or less equal game with my pursuer. I slipped out on one side while he was on the other, and so, aided by several tunnels and several rests, I got at last to a gate at a level crossing; this cut off one part of the island from the other, for here, at this place, a high wire fence stretched north and south.

With vast relief I stooped under the wire, and when I had left my camel, grunting and swearing, some little distance behind, I sat down and began to laugh. It was not, I think, merely hysterical laughter, but rather an upbubbling of gladness that I was alive and safe.

As I look back upon that night, it seems that into it had been crowded a good many significant happenings. I had been lifted to the zenith of an impersonal and serene gladness, and plunged to the depths of panic, and in the end I had escaped sound in limb and soul to laugh an uncontrolled and elemental laughter.

A few days after this adventure the races came to an end. Henrietta emerged from his drunken stupor and I was able to get my stores down to the shallow-bottomed ship's boat that I had hired to take them out to the *Shark* where Toby had been left to await our arrival.

Besides the wooden cases full of stores there were bags of flour, spare tents, baskets of fruit and odd things, also casks of water and beer. It was a heavy boatload, and when all was aboard we found it difficult to place ourselves and work the oars unimpeded. Our boat sat low in the water and, as Henrietta remarked, we were facing an inshore breeze which showed every sign of freshening. The distance to go was about five hundred yards. We started at an exceedingly slow pace, and Henrietta, soon finding the work heavy, suggested that we should hoist a sail and tack, using the oars for additional assistance. While we were stepping the mast, we drifted on to a mud-bank, and there might have stuck had I not jumped out to shove the boat off. My bare feet sank a good eighteen inches into the soft, hot mud beneath the shallow water, which was unpleasantly squelchy between the toes.

"Be careful of the water-snakes," grinned Henrietta; but I was pushing with all my energy, and indifferent to anything but getting the boat clear, until I felt slithering eel-like bodies under my feet, and soon after saw three yellow and black water-snakes four feet long, writhing round near the surface, disturbed from their mud-enfolded slumbers.

I got the boat clear and lifted myself aboard. "What beastly looking things! Do they bite? Are they poisonous?"

"They're said to. Haven't tried them myself. They don't bite unless you treads on 'em," Henrietta chuckled.

The shallow waters on each side of us were now swarming with miniature water serpents that had been disturbed by the strokes of the oars and the dragging of the keel through the thick mud. They had the typical *elaps* appearance with tails vertically compressed for steering. Later, when I had an opportunity of examining a dead specimen, I thought it looked confoundedly poisonous.

That Henrietta should be merely amused at my danger and ignorant foolhardiness nettled me, and conveyed a picture of my own unimportance. Had I been bitten, it would not have mattered; he might even have been glad of a quick end to this tedious job. I looked for some few minutes, with an equal distaste, on my companion, the muddy water, and the writhing sea-snakes.

On the next tack we were free of the mud-bank, but now it became apparent that the wind was freshening considerably, and that our boat, having no keel, was making a lot of leeway. We made little forward progress, and had to measure our approach to the anchored cutter not in minutes, but in hours. At the end of two hours of hard work, we had come most of the way, but had shipped a lot of water. The sea was choppy, and splashed half-bucketsful over the low-riding bulwarks. It was almost impossible to bale in the overcrowded boat, and the unwelcome fact became clear that we were likely to fill and sink.

I made what signs I could to the man in the cutter that we were in difficulties. It was impossible to shout against the wind. In answer to these signals, Toby floated a rope, with a small buoy at the end of it, for our assistance. If we could reach this buoy, we could in a short time pull ourselves up, but unfortunately the rope was not very long, and although we passed several times within a few feet of the buoy, we could never get hold of it. All our frantic tackings and pulling at the oars always brought us a few feet short, for our leeway was worse than ever, and it was obvious that in a very short time we should fill with water.

This was not a pleasant prospect, for the bay was notoriously full of sharks, and, should we founder, there would be the alternative of a swim of some eighty yards against a head sea, or the far longer passage towards the mud and the sea-snakes. For myself, I had decided to swim towards the cutter, but I did not like the idea, nor, to judge from his language, did my companion.

Sudden and ruthless, this danger had arisen. This was a perfectly normal ordinary sort of day, yet it seemed it might be my last. What indeed was to be done? We were making no headway, and certainly we should founder in a very short time.

Toby had at last seen and realized our predicament. He did the only thing that could be done; ran up the jib, lifted anchor, and drifted down upon us, risking the shallow water. Now we were able at last to catch the buoy with our boat-hook; the cutter dropped anchor again, and we pulled up alongside, only just in time to get clear of the submerging boat. As we scrambled on to the deck, the boat, relieved of our weight, remained floating but awash, with all her cargo floating within her.

From this vantage of safety we could afford to laugh, and it was easy to salvage our stores. The day was bright and with a fresh and pleasant wind, it now seemed—when we no longer had to struggle against it. The world was once more as amiable as it had always been.

During the journey back we tacked against a head wind, not arriving at the island till after dark. Henrietta let me sail for most of the time, and then when the wind sank, began to tell tales of the pearl fishing and the pearl smuggling further up the coast. He had been a diver in his youth, and he knew a lot about the islands of the north. On some of them, he said, white men had never landed; the natives were very hostile.

Our stores were welcome, and had not been much damaged by their submersion. The bags of flour that had gone underwater were dry inside, the moisture having soaked only a short way in.

One morning, when I went down for my before-breakfast bathe, I found Louis with a full-grown turtle, about five feet across the carapace, that he had managed to turn over on its back. His idea was that we should kill it, since we were short of fresh meat. We had strong, large knives and ropes, and imagined, in our ignorance, that killing a turtle might take half an hour or so. It took all three of us most of the day, and even when we had its ventral plate off and it was altogether disembowelled, the steaks of meat that we cut off continued to crawl about on the rocks, still showing a life of their own. The front flippers, still attached to the carapace, continued to flap slowly to and fro. When at sundown the dreadful deed was done, we looked and felt like blood-stained savages. To compensate for our own shame, which we did not admit to one another, we gave the natives gifts of meat and eggs and fat, which delighted them.

The turtle soup that is supposed to be so good, and that so few of us taste, is made from the layer of soft green fat that lies just under the shell. We scooped it out in handfuls and gave it to the natives who gulped it down raw. There was enough to make gallons of soup. We tried to make some ourselves, but we must not have diluted it sufficiently, for we found it sickeningly rich. I think the natives did also, for they did not come for second helpings. I could not say at what stage of its dismemberment the turtle died, but the heart went on contracting with great perseverance long after it was cut out and altogether detached.

In Carnarvon I had bought some ten-inch nails; these when sharpened and fitted on to shafts made good fish-spears. When we were bathing in the bays on the eastern coast we took our spears, and waited until a shoal of fish appeared in the shallow water. We never had to wait long, for the shoals were numerous. Without taking precise aim we hurled our spears, and the chances were that we would transfix a fish. The fishes of the sea were our chief food, and most of them seemed good to eat, from the slender garfish to the snappers that we caught on rod and line. In the rock pools were large crayfish, very similar to lobsters in appearance but with smaller pincers. These we were keen to get, but they were not easy to catch, since we had no suitable nets. Many of the molluscs, besides the oysters, were excellent when cooked. There were all kinds of creatures, crabs in scores, sea-worms and holothurians—black, slug-like creatures, inert, almost like vegetables. The natives slit them open and dried them in the sun; they liked them partly decomposed. The sea, besides being the source of most of our food, was a great wonder and delight. While Brown was questioning natives about their genealogies, and Louis was preparing our meals, I spent my time part in and part out of the rock pools.

At night the island magic was most potent, for there is about a tropical night a curious feeling of relaxation. The activities kindled by sunlight have ceased, and all living things accept a respite from the brilliance of day. The central ridge of the island stood grey and definite under the night sky, rising in some places to cliffs with headlands and rough boulders, in others bending to smooth sweeps of blown and undulating dunes. Thicket-filled hollows of clumps of spinifex-grass showed white in moonlight against the sand. The house of the stockman and the hospital buildings were dwarfed by high sandhills.

At the north point of the island there was a long flat beach where turtles came to bury their eggs, and close along the break of the waves was a whitish-pink ridge composed entirely of shells. It was pleasant to shuffle my feet in the surf, and listen to the many mingled small noises. This point was an enchanted place where probably no man had walked before.

We had during our stay on the island an extraordinary, exciting and even dangerous experience. In this region, although the climate is usually hot and fine, there occur, at certain seasons, hurricanes which are called by the white Australians Cock-eyed-Bobs or Willie-Willies. Against the onslaught of these storms all houses, huts or bungalows are firmly chained to the underlying rock. The chains go over the houses, holding them down. Besides the ordinary windows to each dwelling, there are stout wooden shutters that can be fitted at the first warning of a hurricane.

It had been exceptionally hot, still weather for some days. One morning we noticed that waves larger than usual were breaking on the beaches. Brown saw that our barometer had fallen from thirty to twenty-eight. Dr. Hicksey, who was staying on the island at the time, advised us to strike our tents and come into the hospital buildings until after the storm.

We did this with reluctance; then we went down to the beach and had a swim while the waters were still calm. Each oncoming wave presented a smooth satin-like surface to dive through. The natives and the patients at the hospital were all nervous and perturbed, and most of those who usually slept in the dune-hollows came inside, but not all. We took precautions to make the chains secure and to shutter all windows.

The storm came in the late afternoon with sudden fury, driving great waves high up the beach. With the first onrush of wind I could see through the flurry of spray and driven sand the annex to the main building, a flimsy construction whirled away, as it seemed, into the sky, beds and sick natives tumbled in a mass. The next I knew was that I found myself lying flat on the floor, struggling to get my breath. All energies were centred on breathing without sucking down too much sand. The building stood, though it trembled, and through every crack and cranny sand and spray were driven in. After a while I began to believe that the building might go on standing. Myself and the doctor and Louis got on to our knees, and finally stood up, a little ashamed at our first instinctive impulse to lie down. Needless to say the lamp had blown out, and was certainly no longer on the table.

Next came rain in a deluge, slashing against the boards and making the roof thunder above us. We waited; there was nothing else to do. The building creaked, and the storm roared by; the lightning flashed so bright that, although the windows were boarded, light came through cracks sufficient to illumine our pale faces.

At times the wind veered and then it did seem that our shelter would be blown away, for every board in the walls had to re-adjust to the changing pressures. What would happen if it did so, and where would we all be? This question was answered in the morning when the wind subsided. The natives in the annex, that had gone with the first onslaught, had all picked themselves up and crouched in any declivity that they could find. One or two had cuts from flying splinters, but no one was seriously hurt. The same might have been our fate, yet I was glad that the walls and the chains had held so well.

By noon next day both wind and rain had ceased. A gentle breeze ruffled the big rollers that came pounding in and we all swept the sand out of the hospital and shook the blankets. We were in high spirits, as though the Cock-eyed-Bob had done us good; certainly the air was fresh and well-washed. Our tents were pitched again and our work under the big fly-sheet re-established.

The time came when the work at Bernier Island was nearly completed. A short journey to Dorre Island where the women's camp was near the main hospital, was indicated. I did not find it as attractive as Bernier, but it is always interesting to explore new territory. The women of all ages gathered there seemed to have more freedom to wander about the island than the men had on Bernier. Perhaps their spirit of exploration and adventure was stronger. We did not stay there long but one episode stands out vividly in my memory.

I was alone and had gone northward along the coast, and was some distance from the encampment when I came on two young women. They looked little more than girls. They were both stark naked, not even with a string of beads, and they were vigorously engaged in dismembering a large turtle. Their instruments were pieces of broken glass from a bottle. It must have been quite a job to cut through the leathery skin, but they had succeeded in making a hole through which they thrust their young and shapely arms. They had rummaged about in the interior and pulled out quite a large portion of the insides, parts of which they were cramming into their mouths. They looked thoroughly happy.

A bit abashed at this unusual sight, so primitive and so simple, I stood and watched, while the unfortunate turtle heaved vast sighs and waved its flippers from side to side. The girls shouted to me what might have been friendly or happy greetings, but knowing how long it takes to kill a turtle, and being, I admit, a bit embarrassed by the nakedness of these blood-stained young creatures, I decided this was not my affair, and left them to their orgy.

Soon afterwards we returned to Bernier Island to strike our camp, and then back to the mainland with our note-books filled with genealogies, and my collecting-cases with specimens.

FOUR

Exploring Australia

BEFORE LEAVING THE NORTHWEST, we went a short
expedition up the Gascoyne River. It is marked large as a
river on the map, and at the rainy season, I was told, a
considerable volume of water rushed down from the inland uplands, deep enough to tempt sharks and other big sea fish to swim
inland, doubtless in pursuit of smaller fish. During the dry season
the river dried up and became a gravel-strewn ravine, with pools
of various sizes marking its course. The surrounding country in
the neighbourhood east of Carnarvon was arid steppes of semi-
desert, and during the dry season each of these pools became a
centre of animal and vegetable life. In the smaller pools the water
was stagnant, covered by a green scum; the larger ones were
sometimes as much as a hundred yards long or more and in these
I have seen sharks' fins cutting the surface and have had glimpses
of other large fish such as sawfish and sword-fish. These sea
monsters must stay where they are till the next heavy rainfall
washes them back to the river mouth and the sea. Many are found
dead in dried-up pools, and I have seen the snouts of sword-fish
and sawfish decorating the walls of farmhouses a hundred and
fifty miles inland.

To these pools came many animals: kangaroos, wallabies,
boody-rats, bandicoots. Rats and mice were to be seen in the
twilight creeping out from the bushes that surround the pools.
Besides the usual undergrowth, there were frequent groves of tall
gum-trees that marked the river's course.

The eucalyptus gums, which sometimes grow to great heights,

were each possessed by their own animal populations. One had only to lie in the shade and look up to see the tree-lizards clinging close to the smooth, sleek-barked branches. There were tree-mice also and birds of various kinds, but the insects were the most numerous. When the gums were in flower—they do not flower every year but only occasionally—the pink and red blossoms were swarmed about, not only by all kinds and sizes of hymenoptera, but by many sun-flying beetles and butterflies. Huge buprestids whose bronze electra were two inches in length, and lesser ones of burnished green, were to be seen high up, soaring around the flower heads. These most beautiful of all beetles were difficult to capture, as they fly only near the extreme top of the branches. To collect them I was forced to the vandalism of cutting down one of these magnificent trees. It crashed to earth, and with its pink and red blossoms came many of the insects which were drinking their nectar.

Not only on the flowers were creatures of interest found. There were hundreds of species which live under the loose folds of bark: gecko lizards of several kinds, centipedes of all shapes and sizes, some as long as nine inches, orange-coloured and dangerous, with a very poisonous bite; also scorpions, wood-lice and spiders, and hundreds of beetles, round as boot buttons, from the size of a pin's head to a good inch in diameter, and numberless others of different shapes and kinds. But the cicadas were the most noticeable of all, even more than the thousands of biting and stinging ants. They filled the air with their tremendous song, so that the whole earth and all the air vibrated in response to their music. The greatest and the most beautiful of these was a brown, yellow and black insect of three full inches in length, and four and a half inches across the expanded wings. This creature was as large as a small bird, and flew swiftly. On a hot day in the dry season there might well be several hundreds of them singing among the branches of the large trees.

The cicada is a drinker of the tree's sap. It has a sharp sucking beak which it thrusts through the bark of the twigs down to the layer between bark and stem, and while it draws into itself the sweet sap of the tree, it sings. This singing is a harsh, jarring sound when heard close by, but when the insects are distant in the tree-tops, and are pouring out that volume of unchecked ecstasy, then it seems that they are expressing their appreciation and delight in the hot sunlight which gives them life. They create a continuous stream of sound which seems to form a living curtain of gently varying notes enfolding the tree, a curtain which flows to and fro with the moving gusts of air. All through the hours of sunlight they feed and sing, and though many other insects respond to the sun, and become torpid in shadow, the cicada, more than any other creature, appears both in shape and sound to be a direct expression of the sun's heat. Its body is of a dry brittle consistency, and is full of air-spaces; these are re-sonators to the sound box, which is situated just posterior to the attachment of the hind pair of wings. By the opening and the shutting of the doors of these resonators the song is produced.

When the Australian summer is at its hottest, the cicadas mate and lay their eggs high up on the terminal twigs. The female digs with her ovipositor under the bark and tunnels a cell into which she lays from six to ten eggs. Then she passes a little way along the twig and repeats the process. She may lay as many as four hundred eggs, a large family to meet the many risks that must be encountered.

After a few weeks, the eggs hatch. The larvae are at first queer fish-shaped creatures, with large eyes, whose limbs are contained in a sheath which looks like a fin. In this condition they wriggle up out of the cell through the hole left by the ovipositor of their mother. If their limbs were not enclosed in a sheath at this early stage, legs and antennae would become terribly entangled, and they would not be able to get through the hole.

As it is, their legs are safe from entanglement, and they may wriggle and slide amongst one another; they come into the open, though their hinder ends still remain caught in the hole, prevent-ing them from falling. The skin which has enfolded the larva during this emergent stage now splits, and the true larva struggles its way out, held by its hinder end to the integument. It waits for a while, hardening its tender body to the sunshine, then kicks and tests its strength.

The subsequent larval phase is lived under the earth, and there is no future for these tiny aerial fleas, that are born a hundred feet or more from the ground, unless they jump. If they were to linger too long on the tree-tops they would wither and die. They must jump to live; and jump they do in their thousands. I have been under eucalyptus trees when these little flea-like creatures have come showering down, making a pattering and a rustling on the leaves.

Cicadas were to be seen in all parts of Australia. There was a small grey species on Bernier Island, several yellow and orange species elsewhere, but never have I seen such large and magnificently noisy insects as the cicadas of the Gascoyne River.

Our stay on the lower stretches of this dried-up river-bed was not long, but sufficient to implant a vivid picture of the far-reaching waste of desert scrub on each side, filled out by evidence in the silt and debris brought down from inland by the wet-weather floods. Wherever the river flowed, life was abundant, and we were told of the many cattle-stations that attended its long course as far as the Peak Hill district more than five hundred miles inland.

After writing up my notes I turned to find out what I could do about the now extinct tribes of the southwest.

When we look back into the history of the Australian tribes we find that there have been three migrations of aborigines from the northeast. Tribes wandered across the whole width of the continent. The first migrants had a two-class marriage system; they had been pushed by later invasions from the northeast and, at the time of the coming of the white men to Australia, they were confined to the extreme southwest. These tribes had died because they could not sustain the impact of white civilization. The last few survivors lived in a reserve near the small township of Guildford, near Perth, and it was here I heard rumours of a burial ground with a few stakes marking the places of the graves. The last survivor had been buried about fifteen years earlier. They had no relatives to grieve, and their souls had gone to their own happy hunting grounds. Yet I was aware of a prejudice against the opening of graves. First I wanted to find the graves, dig up the skeletons, and bring them safe back to Perth, where I should have to treat the bones, dipping them in glue to prevent further crumbling. This would have to be done in as quiet a way as possible for there was popular indignation caused by a story of a man who had shot a native because he wanted his skull. This was probably untrue, but it had created an atmosphere that would not be propitious to the digging up of skeletons.

I was told of an old Irishman who knew the spot. He agreed to come with me and lend his horse and sulky, if sufficiently rewarded.

We waited for a dark night; then, with spades and sacks under the seat of the sulky, we started our drive into the bush.

I was not altogether fortunate in my companion, for when we got to the place, he was overcome with superstitious fears. He imagined he saw the ghosts of the dead natives flitting about in the glimmer of our lanterns, and had he not been more frightened of being alone than with me in that solitary spot, he would undoubtedly have turned tail and left for home. As it was, nothing would persuade him to handle a spade and help dig. His only use was to hold the lantern and this shook and wobbled up and down as he trembled. I set to work alone. The soil was sandy and easily displaced, but it was hard work and I sweated profusely.

At about three feet down I came on boards that had been placed above the corpses. These were an unexpected obstacle as there were four of them, placed side by side, and each was about four feet long. When these were removed the first thing I found was the head of the buried man. The natives bury their dead in a squatting position. There was no flesh, for all had deliquesced in the dry soil, but hair and skin were intact, and the corpses formed natural mummies. I had to break through the outer skin, and each bone that I got free, I put into one of the sacks. It was a rough job, and I broke several of the ribs in getting them free of the soil. The little bones of wrists and ankles were also a trouble. At last I had one skeleton, more or less complete.

The second grave was also boarded, and this was a woman's grave. I was anxious to have the two of them. The bones were more brittle, and I was tired; I did not make such good progress as at the first grave. Furthermore, my superstitious Irishman had retreated nearer the reassuring presence of his horse, and I was a bit afraid that he would desert me altogether. Fortunately he was too frightened to run away.

It was past midnight when I began hurriedly to fill in the holes. With my Irishman, now restored to confidence, I returned tired but triumphant to the hotel at Guildford. No one was stirring at that early hour. I carried up the sacks to my room and pushed them under the bed. Then I had a bath, got into bed, and slept soundly, far too tired to let the stench of the bones keep me awake.

When I arrived with my booty at my friend's house in Perth, he was laughingly surprised that I had so far succeeded in what he thought was rather a rash enterprise. He assigned me an outhouse with a large table on which I could sort out the bones and dip them in glue, to prevent the further crumbling likely to occur on their journey to England. The rough ride in the sulky had already spoiled some of the more friable ribs.

In spite of my precautions to keep the adventure quiet, a rumour had got around that some sort of mischief was afoot against the native graveyard, warmed by the story about the man who had been shot for his skull. Although there was little to support this, the conscience of the white community was waking to the fact that the natives had, in the past, been badly treated. My problem was how to get my bones to England, for I had no intention of taking them with me on the further journeys I was planning. I packed them carefully in a strong wooden case, labelled "Geological Specimens", and with the connivance of a young man, lately engaged as secretary to a Very Important Person, we smuggled them through in the luggage of the V.I.P. What was not known about was not grieved over.

The case was addressed to an uncle of mine in London. Rashly I told him of its contents and he rather stupidly told his young wife, who did not like the idea of having skeletons in her cupboard. She never quite forgave me. However, the bones were not rejected, and were stowed safely in a cellar till I came more than a year later to claim them.

I was already planning my voyage home via the islands of the Pacific Ocean, but Western Australia was attractive in so many ways that I was in no great hurry to leave. I wanted to visit the southwest, which I had glimpsed on my train journey from Albany to Perth, when at a wayside station I had found a climbing sundew plant; this had so pleased me that I decided then to go back to see more of that land of swamps and great trees.

Limestone caves had recently been discovered near Busselton, within the borders of a great National Reserve. The Western Australian government was anxious to make known the attractiveness and beauty of these caves. They were subsidizing, for a limited period, excursions to the caves. The journey south to Busselton, board and lodging for ten days, the train and buggy rides through the forests to the caves, the services of a guide, all were to be given for the moderate sum of ten pounds. I bought a pass ticket that entitled me to all the richness of this variegated and delightful journeying.

Ten of us assembled on the station at Perth, and we were carried by train south to Bunbury where a buggy drawn by two horses and driven by an old man was waiting. Here eight of the party suddenly changed their minds, not liking the idea of crowding into the buggy, and preferring the prospect of waiting for another, which was said to be on its way. For my only companion I had a rather fragile English lady, whom I judged to be about sixty years old. She proved to be a woman of unbounded enterprise and courage. We took our places on the seat behind the driver, and the three of us jogged at a slow pace into what was in Australia called a domain, a huge government reserve where no one might cut trees or shoot animals; I believe one was also not allowed to catch beetles, but I was not sure about that.

The trees of the domain were enormous; they were jarrah, with stems like those which used to decorate advertisements for Australian wines. They grew in magnificent array, well-spaced and comely. There were so many of these forest giants that their trunks were like the receding, dwindling columns in a temple of infinite dimensions. Our buggy, as it made an ant-like progress under the high canopy of branches through which the sunlight fell in dappled patterns, was dwarfed to a child's plaything.

For hours we had been under the shadow and had paused to water the horses and to stretch our legs. The driver produced a basket of food, thoughtfully provided by the government. He kindled a fire and boiled water for tea. After we had eaten, we lay on our backs for a while, gazing up into the clear spaces of air contained among the branches, and felt the invisible emanations of the forest. Here amongst the great trees was a different spirit from the arid daemon of the northern bush. Streams trickled and gurgled; sometimes a river was to be forded, and our track wound often from a direct course to avoid swamps and fallen tree-trunks.

I do not remember what we talked about. I only remember that our interests ran in common; we both took notice of birds and beasts and plants, and found an ever-increasing pleasure in the scene. In the early afternoon we came into the valley of a small river. This we followed to a clearing where cattle pastured, and to a farmhouse, with a ridge of sand dunes beyond and a sight of the sea. This was our destination; here we were to stay, and from here, on the following days, make journeys to the caves.

The farm was called "Cattle Chosen", and our host and hostess, who were both descendants of the original settlers, told us the story of its origin and of its name. When the first English colonists came to Australia, many of them had only the vaguest idea of the sort of conditions they were going to find. Many brought with them the accustomed conveniences of civilization, things which would be of little use to settlers in a virgin forest, such as family coaches, whose owners fondly imagined that they would be able to drive from place to place in the new continent. There were no roads, and on the west coast few harbours. Many of the ships were run ashore on the beaches, and cargoes landed as best they could be. Men, women and children, horses and cattle, coaches, carts and household goods, were littered along the seaboard. The settlers slept in the coaches and rigged up table-cloths, sheets and blankets as protection from the sun's heat. The cattle and horses strayed; some were lost, some found good pastures. Cattle had found this particular site, and when the owners followed and saw the good grass, the little river and the pleasant prospect, they built their farm and called it "Cattle Chosen". Parts of the original structure were still doing service; they had been added to and enlarged, but always in a fairly primitive manner. The dividing walls of the rooms were made for the most part of hessian, and my travelling companion, whose bedroom was next to that of our driver, declared that every time he turned over in bed the wall shook and she herself responded to the vibrations. It was a house conditioned by its remoteness from the sources of orthodox building material, but a most delightful place where we fed on the best farmhouse fare, and on melons, peaches and figs.

On one side was the forest, and on the other was the river which, as it met the sands, divided into several streams. Beyond the dunes were rippling sea waves lapping a shell-strewn beach. I was well accustomed to shell-strewn beaches, but had never seen one so rich in brilliant colours or decorated by more variegated shells. Here were cowries of many kinds and sizes, the delicate Venus-ear shell, tritons' horns, brilliant pectens, bivalves mirroring every shade of sunset and sky, opercula, pink, mauve and orange, and every one of these sea-shells was only a dead fragment of things that had once lived. Many were already broken, but many were perfect, newly washed from the sea. They were crowded together, streaking the beaches with their vivid tints. Some were in the wash of the clear waters of the streams, some washed by the waves. Every tide the patterns were changed, but always the patterns were there.

During our stay we made expeditions to various caves in the limestone hills not far distant. The rock had been penetrated by underground streams; water had worked along the joints, and run in small tunnels, and after thousands of years had excavated large cavities; then, slipping to a lower level, the water had repeated the process and made other passages, until at last it had found its way to the sea. The empty waterways are the present-day caves, and the whole area of that extensive limestone plateau was probably laced by ancient river-channels. The man who had discovered the caves was an enthusiast and a lover of all that pertained to rocks and underground explorations. Cave-hunting was his hobby, and the government had been wise in choosing him as warden of that part of the domain.

There was no outward trace of the large caves; in the wild wooded country on a flat plateau, the only signs were small holes in the rock, a foot or two in diameter. Some of these were mere pot-holes a few feet in depth, and silted at the base with fine muddy sand. In these I found collections of the bones of small mammals that had probably gone there to die. Some of the holes led down to openings in the rock ten feet wide, and others thirty or more. The floors of these larger but superficial caves were inches thick in stalagmite, in which I found bones of kangaroos and diprotodonts embedded. These bones were extremely difficult to chip out, but I managed to get some specimens.

The stalagmite display was not, at these upper levels, anything remarkable, and our guide led us further and deeper. We climbed down rope-ladders into a darkness of unknown depths. Sometimes our guide led us along underground galleries, loosening, as we went, a string clue, that we might be able to find our way out from that maze of dividing ways. For illumination we carried small lanterns, but when, at the lower levels, we came to features that he considered worthy, he would ignite a tray of magnesium dust and reveal the stalactites and stalagmites, pointing to their perpendicular lines in the silence of their remote loveliness. In one place, a shallow underground lake, about fifty yards long by twenty wide, was supported on what had been at one time the floor of a river. It was now left suspended, and an empty river-bed went beneath. Along this our guide waded to the other end of the lake, where, peering over the lip of the basin, he lit his magnesium flare. From the cave roof, which was about four feet above the lake, pointed hundreds and thousands of thin delicate columns of white calcite. These, in the silver glare, were a fairyland of wonder. Flare after flare was burnt with prodigal extravagance that we might see to advantage this best of his finds.

Climbing back was an arduous task. Sometimes we swayed on the rope-ladder over dark space; sometimes we crept up the face of dripping rocks. At one ledge where we were resting the guide drew my attention to a cylinder of wood thrusting through the stone. It was the root of a gum tree, one hundred and sixty feet underground, an inch and a half in diameter, and going how much further we could not tell.

Often we did not go so deep or so far, but made only short descents. Our guide encouraged me to go alone, to douse my light and sit solitary in darkness. "You will find out what silence is," he said, "not so silent as you think at first. You will find out."

I followed his advice, being careful to take my clue of unwinding string, for the passages continually twisted and branched. When I was deep underground I put out my lamp. No least sound from the earth's surface penetrated, no air stirred. It was more silent than the stillest valley, the remotest mountain-top. Then, as the minutes passed, I began to hear a noise; it was a pushing, pulsating rhythm; it was quite loud, and seemed to grow louder. I spoke so as to dispel it, but it came back; it seemed almost to be within my own head. So it was; it was the sound of blood near my eardrums, a sound which must always be present, but so faint as ordinarily to escape notice. It could only be heard when all the outer noises were stilled. This was the process of my own living, and I did not like it. The insistence was repulsive, overwhelming me with the activity of my own being.

Our guide was a naturalist by nature, a man of sensitive observation who had spent many years in the bush and had devoted much ingenuity to the exploration of caves. As warden he received a salary, and was free to explore to his heart's content, and to develop and make accessible those caves which he had already found. During the time we spent together we discussed many subjects, including the manner of birth of kangaroos and some of the smaller marsupials. His personal observation did not match altogether with the most generally accepted accounts. I had not read, at that time, nor do I think they were published, Dr. Wood Jones' conclusions. I am sure my friend the warden would have been interested to read them. Besides teaching me many things pertaining to Australian bush life, he confided a dream of adventure and treasure-seeking.

In the early days, when the Dutch claimed the west coast of New Holland, a ship carrying bullion for the payment of soldiers was lost with all hands somewhere between Cape Mantelle and Cape Naturalist. My friend had discovered, in a muddy estuary not far from the caves, a ship corresponding to its description. The dismasted hull lay embedded in the mud. He supposed that the Dutch vessel had been swamped and driven ashore, and that in all probability the gold bullion was still in the hold. Would I care to have a look? He could take me to the place at low tide.

The ship was there all right, though not very much of her was above the surrounding swamp. At low tide we clambered aboard. The deck appeared to be intact, though all the hatches were filled full of mud, which had sifted in, tide after tide, and now probably filled every hollow space. The boat lay a good half-mile inland from the coastline, and a thick tangle of vegetation had grown into that region where the salt and fresh water met. The tides would be the chief obstruction to any attempt at salvage, for she could not be dug out if water was always sweeping in. One might break in the deck and dig out the silt, but that was likely to be a tough job. Unfortunately neither he nor I had any money available.

When I returned from the limestone caves and the bathing beaches of "Cattle Chosen" I still lingered a few days in Western Australia. At that time, fifty years ago, the bush between Guildford and the Darling Ranges was still much as it had been from the time that the first white men came to Perth. On the marshy flats were cirex stumps that had survived many bush fires. Their exteriors were burnt black, and for this reason they were known as "black-boys", the only reminders of the fires they had survived. Their centres sprouted spiky leaves. Around on the swampy ground were a great variety of flowers, from tiny orchids and climbing sundews to the black kangaroo paws, with grevilleas and many bushes of he-oak and she-oak. It was here that I searched for a curious, insignificant but exceedingly interesting little animal that possessed characteristics both of the mollusca (slugs and snails) and of the jointed animals, like insects and crabs.

The creature was called *Paripatus*. It was jointed like a caterpillar in so far that it had a number of legs, although there was no external sign of segmentation. It had eyes like a worm at the end of horns like a snail's horns. Many of its inside organs were like those of a slug; altogether it looked like the survival of some ancestral form.

I was most anxious to find these creatures and bring home specimens bottled in spirit. At first I looked in vain, and then suddenly it seemed that I got tuned-in to them, through long hours of concentration. I found first one, then another, and then they seemed to be under every damp log that lay in a marshy spot. While I was hunting for these creatures, I was silent and absorbed in the search, and I seemed to the creatures of the bush no more dangerous than an old stump. On several occasions small groups of kangaroos came springing by. They came on me suddenly, paused, had a good look, and passed on. There were parrots, black with pink under the wings, and sometimes the handsome cockatoo that was really not white but cream-coloured. There were frequent flights of green parakeets and the common red crows that were to be found in most parts of Australia. There were wallabies and boody-rats, small climbing kangaroo rats, a vast number of frogs, and some large toads that, when evening came, made a noise like the drawing of a cork that merged into the thrumming of a bass string. There were snakes and many lizards, mice and tree-frogs and innumerable insects, among them huge dragonflies which drove away the clouds of biting flies.

The time came to say a reluctant goodbye to Western Australia. Before sailing I had put in a couple of weeks at a job in a brewery, cleaning out barrels, and so had replenished my fund of money; also I had received some from Europe. I bought a second-class fare on one of the older of the Orient-line boats. She had a reputation for rolling, and, to add to this discomfort, she sailed from Albany with a distinct list to starboard.

To be on a large ocean-going steamer is always pleasantly exciting. A steamer is like a small city, with captain for king. Second-class passengers do not see much of him, but they know he is there, and can admire from a distance his assurance in command. There was nothing very remarkable about the voyage, except that I shared a cabin with a lawyer, an undertaker and a parson—all that was necessary to prepare a man for his hereafter. The hereafter seemed at one time very near when we struck a northerly gale in the Bight. I mentioned our ship had a list to starboard, and now a gale of great force struck our port side.

Each time we rolled, everything that could move shot away into the scuppers, and then with the next roll shot back again. On deck we clung to anything available and in the cabin at night, I lay in my bunk while my large cabin trunk shot to and fro with every roll. At the end of each starboard roll the ship trembled as though uncertain whether it should recover or turn turtle. Sometimes this period of trembling would last for as much as ten seconds, then hesitatingly she would swing back. I was made additionally nervous by knowing that a few weeks earlier a large ship, plying on the western coast, had turned turtle. She had completely disappeared, and all that was found of her was a door washed off the steward's pantry.

We arrived in Sydney none the worse for the gale, and here again I was lucky in having introductions to friends, who gave me generous hospitality. Sydney, as it was then, seemed teeming with an almost explosively joyous life. It was a lovely city on the shores of a superb bay, with tough-looking men, wonderful swimmers, and a great many pretty girls, as tough, perhaps, as the young men.

Thousands of pictures present themselves as memory-images: crowded tram-cars screeching up and down the hilly landscape, each car crammed with people hanging on like flies, not controlled as in England, but left to survive as chance willed. Those who could not get inside or on top got a foothold, or handhold, and swung in the air at the sharp corners, sometimes dropping off, and no one caring.

There were bathing reserves, staked against the sharks, which in Sydney are much more dangerous than in Shark's Bay; they are blue sharks, and often very large. Here were men and girls in smart water-attire, swimming and diving as only Australians and Polynesians can swim and dive, always laughing. Here you could have a face-to-face conversation with a man-eating shark, the shark on one side of the stakes and you on the other. Here I caught and handled the elegant hippocampus, exquisite little fishes that look like a cross between a knight chessman and a small fish.

There was sailing in any sort of boat from a dinghy to a yacht.

Many beautiful creeks could be explored, and from off shore there was a view of city buildings, half-hidden in mist and smoke. Overboard great jelly-fish, as big as tubs, floated by, yellow and brown and forever pulsating.

There was an attractive botanic garden that had held its place, right in the middle of the city, although close-pressed by surrounding buildings; it retained the quality of a small tropical island, with many strange plants and a population of lizards, butterflies, beetles and huge centipedes.

In the Chinese quarter one could buy small crocodiles, lizards and tree-frogs, and queer things to eat and drink. Not far distant were the crash and roar of the traffic in George Street, and the great buildings, symbols of wealth and power.

I bought a ticket to Blackheath in the Blue Mountains. On the journey I was disappointed that I could see no mountains. The train puffed up a slow incline, and on getting out at the top, I saw only flat country; but after I had left the village and walked into the bush I got my first glimpse of azure emptiness as I looked into one of the great clefts that justify the name of the Blue Mountains.

These are not mountains in the ordinary sense of the word. They have come into being in a peculiar way. Once what is now the flat surface of the mountain plateau (never much more than two thousand feet high) was the bottom of an ocean; in the course of geological ages it has been raised up and now, just as a mud-surface cracks when it dries, this once flat bottom of prehistoric sea has cracked in clefts proportionately large. These clefts in places are enormous, as much as half a mile across, though often much less. When one comes suddenly on the edge of such a cleft the effect is wonderful, for it goes down two thousand feet deep, and is often an abrupt drop. Far down below through the azure blue atmosphere one can see the tops of the forest trees, and distant rivers. Huge tree-ferns look like tiny rosettes, and below are eagles circling.

The Australian government has in some places built long stairs that creep close to the cliffs, and these lead down, for whoever likes to climb so far, into the valley lands at the bottom. The streams that flow at the upper level spill over the edges of the precipices, and as they fall are twisted and swirled about by air currents into curtains of spray which sway in the breeze, as sunlight makes rainbows through and about them.

I have climbed in the Alps, seen the mountains of New

Zealand and Fiji, lived on the West Australian plateau, crossed
the Rockies of Canada, and looked down on the Nile Valley from
the top of the Great Pyramid, but never have I met anything to
compare with the beauty and grandeur of the canyons in the Blue
Mountains of New South Wales. They are not distinctively high,
but the marvellous blues of these deep ravines, the swirling
falling waters and the eagles so far below give a feeling of
something not of this world.

I was at once enchanted, and because I had become accustomed
to sleeping out in odd places, I was not content to sleep in any
house or hotel; I brought a couple of blankets and a ground-sheet
to a suitable cranny at the top of a precipice. When the cicadas
had ceased their sunshine singing, many frogs of various kinds,
some in the trees, some from mossy banks of streams, began their
songs. A few birds chirruped late into the twilight, bats began
to fly, owls hooted, some of their voices coming from far below.

I had a few wonderful nights on the Blue Mountains, and in the
mornings, at the first dawn, I wandered about, taking in all I
could of the exceeding strangeness. Sometimes in the early
morning the air was clear overhead, while down in the valleys all
was mist and the swirling surface of clouds. As the sun rose, and
its heat struck both uplands and valleys, the clouds below seemed
to boil and bubble and break, and then reform. They came
seething up out of the grey, thick mists, and under the sun's
touch scattered into plumy fragments, revealing an underworld
of distant forest and river and rainbow lights in curtains of spray.

Such experiences justify all the discomforts of travelling,
compensate for all the mosquito bites, the moths that buzz in
one's ears, the stinging of ants, and other insect plagues, including the inquisitive little tree-frogs that were so common that they
got into my blankets and into my hair while I slept. To be alone
on the edge of a precipice, to watch how clouds were made and
unmade, to listen and to watch: this was exceedingly good. Yet
sometimes, with a pang, I thought of England, of the North and
South Downs, of the English butterflies that I loved better than
any foreign ones, and I wished that I could be home.

I returned to Sydney and the sea-bathing, and the preparation
for the next jump-off. My plans were already made for a journey
to one or other of the South Sea Islands, either Fiji or Samoa.

This was before either of the great wars, and the South Sea Islands still held the glamour of the unexplored. There were islands and districts little known to what we look on as civilization. Since I had had so close a relationship with some of the wild Australian tribes of the northwest, I now hoped to find out what life was like in Polynesian villages. However, there were other places I wanted to see before I left Australia.

South of Sydney, in the neighbourhood of the township of Kiama, were basalt rocks which offered the same sort of formations as those of the Giant's Causeway in Ireland. I was well rewarded for the journey; the scenery at that time was wild and strikingly picturesque. The cliffs of black basalt, in the process of cooling many hundreds of thousands of years ago, had cracked in a regular and characteristic way called "jointing". The joints were so arranged as to form somewhat irregular hexagons made of close-fitting portions, one on top of another, and in close columns. The "bricks" of each column varied in size, sometimes only a few inches thick, sometimes several feet. In diameter the pillars varied from fifteen to twenty inches. Seen from a distance the exposed cliff surfaces had the appearance of a gigantic clustering of black and imposing columns.

In the cliff-face were caverns and caves of all sizes which had been formed by the falling away of broken-off jointings of rocks. At high tide the sea entered the larger caverns, and the constant pressure of advancing and retreating waters had extended them inland to surprising distances from the shore. Standing on the cliff one could hear the sea sucking and plunging far beneath in the tunnels of these caverns. The constant movement of the waves had caused large blow-holes, sometimes as much as half a mile inland, where sea spray was ejected to nearly forty feet high. In such places the falling sea-water had killed the land plants, leaving black basalt rocks exposed, flecked with white foam. From these blow-holes came roarings and rumblings from deep down, and now and then explosions as the spray was shot exceptionally high. These displays were, of course, at their best when the tide was high and backed by a wind off the sea.

I wished I could have stayed longer at Kiama, but as usual I had to consider how much money I could spare for such side-excursions, and how much to keep in hand for the eastward journey. I regretted having to leave before going down to some of the smaller caves in the upper cliff-face; these were inhabited by

several kinds of bats, and I would have liked to get specimens of
their fleas.

To the north of Sydney, the New England Ranges run roughly
north and south; the uplands rise to three thousand feet, forming
a wide plateau of rolling pasture well suited for rearing cattle and
sheep. I was given an introduction to a farmer who would take me
as a paying guest, whose station was situated on this plateau about
three hundred miles north of Sydney. The opportunity of
experiencing another kind of life was too good to be missed, and
taking the minimum amount of luggage, I set out. I had been given
to understand that the new life would involve a good deal of
riding, and I was advised, when asked if I knew how to ride, to
say that I did not but that I would like to learn—this in spite of
the fact that I had ridden many kinds of horses since I was ten
years old. This would give me a better chance, my adviser told
me, of not having my neck broken, for if I said with any confidence
that I could ride, I might be provided with some buck-jumper or
rooter that only an experienced Australian could deal with. I took
this advice to heart.

I was met by my host at Armidale, and we drove in his sulky to
the farm about twelve miles distant. It was a series of low one-
storey buildings that had been put up at various times, as the
farm had grown and prospered. The kitchen, and all that went
with it, was separate from the main buildings, and was built out
of empty kerosene tins. They make good building material, for
the air-space inside them keeps out the heat of the sun. They
formed only the outer walls; inside there was another wall, made
of a stamped metal popular at that time in Australia called
"wunderlich".

I was introduced to the family. There was the farmer and his
wife, a son of about my own age, twenty-six years, two daughters
eighteen and sixteen, and a boy of ten. There were ten dogs of the
lurcher or collie type. These were extremely well regimented and
controlled, not only by their master but by the boss-dog, who
was an exacting tyrant and bully. They were so well accustomed
to herding cattle and sheep, that when off-duty the boss-dog
herded all the others. They hated it, but submitted.

I soon found out that riding was the order of the day. I had not
made any such crass mistake as to bring riding breeches, for these

would have been considered the height of affectation. Blue, hard cotton dungarees, tied below the knee and at the instep, were the correct dress. And sure enough I was asked whether I could ride. I twigged that the older boy was waiting with some interest for my answer. I shook my head sadly, but said I thought I might not be too long in learning.

A dun-coloured horse, standing about fifteen hands, was allotted me. He treated me kindly after two small bucks to make sure I was in the saddle. After that the three of us rode out to look for, and bring in, a flock of sheep.

The country of the east Australian uplands was used mostly at that time for grazing; much of it was salt-bush and small scrub, well fitted for fattening sheep. The enclosures on the upland farms were often several square miles in extent; when a farmer went to look for his sheep he went on a horse, and it might well be some time before he got sight of his distant flock. Mounted beside the farmer, I could hardly claim to be a helper, but was an admiring spectator of the rounding-up. Halting at times and standing in our stirrups to get the farther view, we gazed into the violet-blue shimmering distances of salt-bush. Everywhere was a haze over the sun-stricken flats; in the foreground the blue fleshy-leaved bushes clustered close to the salty, black earth, and in the distance what looked like pools of water floated here and there in the hazy air, a little raised above the surface. These might vanish as one looked, and appear in some other place.

At length the distant flock was seen—difficult enough even from our raised position on horseback—and then began the task of the dogs. The sheep on the big runs were not half as tame as our English sheep; if one had ridden towards them, they would have retreated indefinitely into farther distances. Two or more dogs were usually employed for rounding up a flock, and it was their task to bring the sheep towards us, and then when within range of further instructions, to drive them as directed. The dogs, being on the ground, could not of course see the sheep, but they could see the farmer, and they knew how to interpret his gestures and the shrill whistles he gave.

First was a short whistle to draw their attention. Then, pointing in the direction of the flock, he would whistle again. The dogs set off, not in the direction of the flock, but away at right angles to where their master had pointed. Soon they were out of sight, and for the next ten or fifteen minutes we must wait. At length, the flock could be seen in motion, and now we could ride towards it; as soon as the dogs were within earshot further orders were given. Falling in behind the flock, we went towards the pens, and here, through a system of hurdled spaces getting ever smaller, the sheep were driven till they were close packed against one another. Men now waded in amongst them for the "culling", as it is called —the picking out of either the better or the worse. This was hard work; the sheep that were culled were seized by their wool and lifted over the hurdles, and so the flock was divided as required, one part being sold to a dealer and the other kept. Lifting the sheep was no pleasant job, for not only was it exhausting to keep at for any length of time, but the hands of men so employed usually got poisoned by small prickly seeds caught in the wool. These sharp-pointed seeds made small wounds, and into these wounds oil and dirt penetrated, causing festering sores which were very painful. Yet in spite of the sores the work had to continue, the heavy struggling sheep still had to be lifted, and thorny seeds continued to prick already sore hands.

The dogs had been taught the uttermost refinements in the art of herding. By way of practice, and in competition one with another, dogs were required to drive three-week-old chicks into an empty kerosene tin. Week-old chicks can run well, yet they must not be driven hard or they soon become exhausted. They must be kept just moving, yet must not be unduly frightened, and they must be herded together, a most difficult task. Often the dog would lie on the ground with forepaws stretched out, and, as he persuaded the chicks in the way they should go, he himself pushed along on his chest, putting out a paw to right or left as necessary, and getting them all, safe and unflustered, into the tin. The winning dog in a competition was the one who could do this in the shortest time.

The herding instinct became an obsession with many of the Australian dogs. When there were no sheep or cattle to herd they would herd the chickens that ran loose in the farmyards; finding them only too easy to hold together in a posse, the dogs discovered that roosters hated to be separated from their hens. To keep a rooster from a hen was not easy. I have watched a dog, nose to nose with a desperate and panting bird, keep up for an hour or more a cruel to-and-fro dance, the rooster trying to get to his hens and the dog forbidding him.

The dry air, the brilliant scorching sunlight, the hard dusty earth: on the upland farms these were the foreground of a vast yonder that stretched in the daytime into violet-blue distances and a haze of heat, and at night into a dim void where the sound of scuttling wallabies and a few bird-voices broke the stillness. The salt-bush country showed little variation; everywhere the scrubby low-growing bushes with small succulent leaves put their roots deep into the black soil. Crusted white salt lay in bands and streaks here and there, and in some localities there were numbers of small round ponds placed almost as regularly, one to another, as the holes in perforated zinc. How these had come to be, and why they persisted, I could not imagine. Their water was shallow and brackish, and though sometimes salt-crusted, was the home of pink and green algae. Wallabies, bandicoots, boody-rats and marsupial mice regularly drank from it, and indeed there was no other water to be had, save occasionally a light fall of dew. On these upland plains, the sheep wandered in semi-wildness and flourished. An almost ideal environment had here awaited their advent. For countless ages it had grown and offered its succulent leaves to the indigenous fauna, and then, with the coming of the white man, had come the Asiatic sheep, first a few and now multitudes; and from the sheep came the tight-gripped bales of wool that went in huge wagons drawn by camels to the ports.

My hands soon got poisoned, and since I was a mere guest, I cried off this exhausting part of a farmer's life. Our work was not all with sheep. In other districts of this enormous farm were less salty areas, with mulga and acacia scrub, something similar to that in the west. On this land were herds of semi-wild horses, and large herds of cattle. It was not considered safe to go on foot, for if one met a herd, they were likely to attack.

My short experience of the work I found exciting; not that I was much assistance, for I found it difficult to ride and keep my horse from dragging in towards the galloping herd of wild cattle. We rode with a snaffle rein and no curb to the bits, for Australian men controlled their horses and steered them almost entirely with their knees. I had at times to use both hands to keep my mount from drawing into the herd. My companions were amused at my incompetence. They were easily able to ride their horses and crack their long whips at the same time. Alec, the farmer's son, was a marvellous rider; he could gallop in front of a galloping herd, and by the pistol-shot cracks of his whip turn them or divide them as he wished. There were tense moments when the cattle stood, uncertain whether to charge, and then turned at an extra crack of the whip.

We were not, of course, galloping to turn them all the time; mostly we were jogging along beside the deep-breathing cattle that jostled one another, each pushing with strong fore-shoulder and heavy horned head. The eyelids drawn back from the bulging eyes exposed brown iris-rims flecked with white and with red veins. These were wild lives, primitive in their fierceness and fear. I found a kind of exultation in being beside them, and feeling the earth shake to the thud of their feet; their strange cow and bull lives were so different from my European heritage. If I were on foot they would kill me, and if I let my horse draw in and get mixed amongst them, my knees would be crushed. My horse was excited by their near presence, and kept flinging up the yellow foam from his mouth.

This was a sample of the life of an upland farmer. I was glad to have had the experience, and yet one more before leaving for the south. There was to be a short overlanding, some three hundred head of cattle to be driven forty miles to another station. It is a slow, tedious business, riding to and fro behind the herd. A cloud of flies buzzes around every living head. Nothing can keep them off; the constant wiping of them away squashes many on cheek and forehead, and their juices begin to make sore places. One man must always be on duty at night, riding slowly round the resting herd. A low continuous noise, either singing or humming, reassures the cattle, and prevents any sudden and single sound that might stampede them. Cattle are easily stampeded in unfamiliar country, and once fear is amongst a scattered herd it is difficult to gather them together again. Also there was the chance that they might overrun our camp. We spent two nights in this way, and three days of trekking, before reaching our destination.

Close to the farmhouse there was a small camp of natives, some of whom gave their services, not for money but for food. The aboriginal men are superb riders, as I saw when we rounded up some three-year-old horses that had run wild in the bush since their birth. These were driven in the same sort of way that the sheep flocks had been driven.

Ultimately, a single horse is driven into a narrow, elongated

space about six feet high on each side, built of boards with spaces
between so that a man can get his hands through easily. When
the young horse is inside, other boards are slid across at the back
so that he cannot get out. Then the horse-breaker begins to talk in
a low and soothing voice. The horse, which has never been so close
to a man before, is sweating with fear. After a while the man will
gently and firmly lay his hand on the horse's shoulder and, if he
can, keep it there for a while. The horse snorts and jumps about,
and the sweat of fear pours from him. Gradually by patting and
talking to and coaxing the creature, it becomes less flustered. A
bridle or a rope is hung over his neck. The next day the procedure
is repeated and he is persuaded to accept a bit and bridle, and, if
things are favourable, a saddle and girth. The next day, or the
next, according to the condition of the horse, he is led out,
bridled and saddled. The Australian saddles have cups into
which a man can thrust his knees. With a quick jump a man is in
the saddle, and his feet in the stirrups.

Then begins a dance; the horse bucks, and roots, and springs
in all directions, but the man miraculously keeps his seat. After a
while the horse must pause from exhaustion. He is patted and
reassured. But the bucking begins again. He again subsides, and
the patting and reassuring words calm him a little.

During the several horse-breakings I saw, the whip was only
used when a horse had the bright idea of lying down and rolling
to rid himself of his rider. The man rose quickly to the occasion;
he was off before the horse was fairly down, and had his hand on
the bit. As the horse rose again he was in the saddle. The
Australian farmers are wonderful horsemen, and especially the
aborigines, for this was the work they liked; I got the impression
that they knew they were even better with difficult mounts than
were the white men.

Life on an Australian cattle-station is hard, but for the men who
live there nothing can be better. They love the ever-present
feeling of the vastness of the bush, and the great size of their
enclosures, their flocks and herds. As the spirit of the western
goldfields has captured men who dig for the precious metal, so
the spirit of these New England Ranges has captured those who
make their homes there. They have become its servants and
worshippers.

I stayed longer than I had intended, yet all the while the
adventure to the Pacific Ocean was calling. I said goodbye to my

Australian bush scrub and nests of white ants

Native house in Fiji (*above*)
Interior of Fijian house (*below*)

kind and tolerant hosts, and returned to Sydney with a feeling that I had learnt quite a lot about horses, and had come to know better than before the many varied aspects of that land, not yet broken in altogether to the uses of men.

FIVE

Fiji

— ✱ —

DURING MY STAY in Sydney I was advised to go first-class to Fiji if I wanted to be well received by the white residents. With this advice, I was given an introduction to a magistrate in Ovalau who might help me in my journeys amongst the native tribes, and another letter, written in Fijian, that would be helpful.

My cabin companion was a Dr. Fox, one of the chief medical practitioners in Suva, who soon after I had made his acquaintance invited me to be his guest. We found plenty of interests in common, since we were students of native life; both were keen naturalists, both believed in magic. Dr. Fox had many stories of the magic practised in Fiji, telling of localities where turtles could be called, of fire-walking, of devil-corpses that screamed in coconut plantations, and of native cures for maladies. In particular he mentioned a kind of ophthalmia, known as "bung-eye", which was common amongst both natives and whites. The eyelids became much inflamed and congested and, in bad cases, the eyeball was completely covered with pus and blood. The affected part was extremely sensitive. He did not know any cure for the complaint, but he knew an old woman witch-doctor who gave the following treatment, and to her he sent his patients. She rested the head of the sufferer on her thigh, then after a few passes and muttered incantations, seized each swollen eyelid and bent it back, scraping the underside with the file-like leaf of the bread-fruit tree. This rough treatment was hardly felt by the patient, whether native or sensitive white woman, who lay in a kind of sleepy drowse. The eyes, when clear of all extraneous matter, were thoroughly washed. The magic, to use the ambiguous word, lay in the presence of the witch-doctor, who could miraculously make almost pleasant an agonizing operation. Some occult relation between disease and witch-doctor effected the cure.

During those few days of our sharing a cabin, Dr. Fox told me much about Fiji. He had begun his sojourn on the islands with a full stock of western prejudices, but facts had changed his viewpoint. He told of fire-walking along a trench containing red-hot stones and glowing embers: no pain, no scorching of feet. He had seen this many times. On one occasion, a Scotsman was staying with him, a daring fellow who asked if he could not walk the stones. His feet were washed and words muttered. He was told that on no account must he look back, but must walk confidently on. The first part of the ordeal went as foretold, but near the end, with only one step to take, the Scotsman half turned his head to test the magic. He immediately felt a burn, but, curiously enough, it was not on his foot but on his buttock, which was far removed from the heat. Dr. Fox treated the burn, which was of considerable size, and painful as all burns are. In some inexplicable way the inhibiting power of the magic had been diverted, striking at random. The natives thought it a great joke.

Latoka was our first port and here an amusing incident occurred. Dr. Fox had for some months been carrying on a feud with the South Steamship Company, which he described as the meanest, most blackguardly concern in the South Seas, which was saying not a little. He was suing them for damages, which they refused to pay in full. It happened that the boat in which we were travelling was heavily laden, her deck-space largely occupied with crates containing iron-ware. Our passage had been over smooth seas, but the ship lay low in the water and had moved with slow and heavy lurches. It seemed likely that she was overloaded.

We tied up at Latoka after dark, and would there unload a good deal of our cargo. Dr. Fox was one of the first down the companionway, and took me with him to witness that the Plimsoll line was well under water. He at once took out warrants of arrest against the captain, the chief cook and the chief engineer. The whole boat buzzed with excitement, since this held up further activities. It was generally known that the Company's record was not good. Cable messages were exchanged with Sydney, and within an hour Dr. Fox was offered full satisfaction for the outstanding differences with the Company. This was to be immediately paid in cash in return for his withdrawing his charges. He had won hands down and everyone seemed delighted, including the captain, the cook and the chief engineer, whom the doctor invited to celebrate the occasion with drinks.

At Suva I lived after the manner of an English gentleman, a change from the dusty and unwashed life in the Australian bush. Society on the Islands, so far as the white population was concerned, was divided between Government House, "Business" and "the Beach". My natural place was with "the Beach", but I was included among the elect of Government House. Here, having grown accustomed to the taboos of the aborigines, I recognized the taboos of civilization. The "Business" section included a number of Chinese, many highly educated, cultured and wealthy men. One of these asked me to his aesthetically arranged house, and introduced me to his beautiful wife and no less beautiful daughters. Their simple manners charmed me, and I was particularly pleased when one of the young ladies offered me an ivory stick with a small carved hand at the end, with which I might scratch my back. In their company I felt myself to be a western barbarian.

A great deal of house property in Suva was owned by the Chinese. They and a German company called Marks Brothers competed for the mastery of trade. Before the first war, Germany was gaining influence in British colonies by simple and unwarlike methods. It was possible for German firms to borrow money from their government at one-and-a-half per cent: this no British firm could do. The Chinese work hard and their food is simple compared to that of the European. Also they were extremely punctilious in their trading. If, for example, one wanted a house built by a Chinese firm, an estimate was given of every detail, and, what was exceptional, a date for completion which was adhered to, the day and the hour. The Chinese grew and distributed nearly all the vegetables, apart from native roots and fruits. These they grew under glass, and since they also controlled most of the emptying of earth closets, they had a plentiful supply of manure. Native fruits which grew wild in the jungle were not traded, and while living in the towns I found them almost impossible to buy. I could only get them by walking to nearby villages. There were plenty of oranges that should be eaten while green; after they had turned yellow they were no good.

Of bananas there were a great variety, some very large, pink-skinned, tough and tasteless, but not too bad when cooked. The little yellow ones that grew in clusters were the best for eating raw. These were not sold because they could be picked anywhere. There were pawpaws, which looked like small melons, delicious eaten at breakfast. Their seeds, rich in pepsin, were used for making digestive tablets.

In the bush, I found several kinds of snakes, none of which was poisonous. There were plenty of lizards, especially geckos. These frequented the houses and were welcome visitors since they ate flies, mosquitoes, spiders and centipedes.

For more than a week I stayed with Dr. Fox, but I wanted to put the letter written in Fijian to the test among the chieftains. In Suva I had met a Scotsman to whom the magistrate in Sydney had given me an introduction. He read my letter and smiled, but like the writer refused to interpret. He suggested I should travel the lagoons, visiting the islands scattered between Moturiki and Ovalau. He said he could provide me with a whale boat manned by six convicts under the control of a native policeman. The convicts were constrained under a Methodist-imposed law for the crime of fornication. A large proportion of the young men of the islands had to serve a term at one time or another.

At Latoka there was a delay before my small crew was assembled, and this seemed a good opportunity to use my introduction to the sugar company. I was received kindly, and the local manager gave me a pass allowing me to travel on the railway that connected the plantations. The plantations were manned by Indians who were employed as indentured labour. The wages offered were tempting to Indian peasants, yet there was a good deal of discontent among the field-workers at the time I was there. They had to pay taxes and fees of various kinds, and the wages that looked so good from afar left small margin. The hygienic conditions in the camps were not good, and only one woman for fourteen men was allowed. The district was buzzing with rumours, among them the story that more than one of the white overseers had been waylaid in lonely places and cut to pieces with the heavily loaded matchets used for cutting through the base of the sugar canes. I was surprised, and a bit shocked, to see the overseers mounted on horses, with long whips that they cracked as they rode among the labouring Indians. However, it was not for me as a guest of the company to make remarks. I noted the discrepancy between the missionaries' attitude towards the sexual lapses of native Fijians, and their seeming indifference towards the sugar company's regulation of one woman for fourteen men. Religion did not interfere where business was concerned. The care of the native Fijians appeared to be the special prerogative of the Wesleyan missionaries, as I was to discover in several amusing ways before the end of my stay.

There was a lagoon within a couple of miles of the town, approached by a native path that wound its way through the surrounding jungle of trees and linias, sometimes edged by clumps of sensitive plant that collapsed their leaves at the lightest touch. This lagoon was within the protecting reef and comparatively shallow; it was reputed to be at most times free of sharks. I was conducted thither by a Fijian who knew a little English. When we arrived at the lagoon we found three or four Fijian lads. These were all supremely at home in the clear warm water. In England I had considered myself a good swimmer, but here I saw how truly amphibious men can be. Fijians often venture miles out to sea, regardless of sharks. Sometimes they carry a knife for the purpose of ripping up the shark's belly from heart to vent, but mostly they go unarmed. On the occasion of this, my first visit to a lagoon, I had no other means of communication than the simple phrase "Vanarka, vanarka", which stood for many greetings: "Good morning", "How are you?", "Here I am" and "All is well". I found myself not too badly left behind, until by gestures and shouts I was led to the face of a high coral rock containing a cave into which the lagoon water flowed. We swam in some thirty yards or so, and then suddenly I was alone except for the man who had led me to the lagoon. He laughed and pointed to the base of the rock, then dived, and did not rise again.

I guessed there must be some tunnel under the rock, but how far did it lead? How far would I have to swim under water before being able to rise? I hesitated, then taking a deep breath made the plunge. Sure enough the tunnel was there, and before many strokes I could see a dim green light ahead. When I rose I exchanged my only word of Fijian with the laughing young men who were waiting for me: "Vanarka, vanarka"—"Here I am. All is well." The cavern was illuminated with a lovely green twilight, reflected sunlight rising through the water from the white coral floor of the cave. There was a little ledge on which we could stand with head and shoulders above water. Here we rested, and conversed, I talking English and my companions their native tongue. I learned it was better to talk boldly on, rather than remain tongue-tied. Words not understood still somehow conveyed meaning.

Returning to Latoka, I went for one more rail trip with a member of the sugar company; I asked him why no Fijians worked for the company. "They are too well off," he said, "they don't like work. They have no ambition. They have all the riches they need. The sea provides them with fish and the jungle with roots and fruit, and the coconut trees give both meat and drink. All the work a Fijian has to do is to plant a coconut once a year; there are plenty of young palms growing all the while." He told me that the natives were protected by law from selling their land to any unauthorized white man. This had been deemed necessary in the early days of their primal innocence. Why indeed should they sell their labour and undertake arduous tasks? They did, however, become proficient as policemen.

At Suva I was advised to visit the island of Mbau; until quite recently this had been a stronghold of cannibalism and a terror to the neighbouring coast villages. On this island were many relics of the savage past that were rapidly disintegrating, and well worth seeing. A small paddle-steamer plied from Suva across the bay to the mouth of the Rewa river, up the river for ten miles until a branch joined it from the east, then up the canal to its outlet not far from the island of Mbau. These were tidal waters, and the journeys were planned to catch the tides. It was not unusual for the little steamer to be stranded on some mud-bank, where it would have to wait with its impatient passengers, and this in fact happened to me. We came slowly to a stop with the churning of paddles and upchurning of the river-bed. The engines no longer turned, and we settled comfortably into the mud.

Our boat's complement consisted of the captain, a German of vast experience in coastal cruising, an engineer, and a deck-hand. There were three male passengers, including myself, and there was also the captain's half-caste wife. After it was clear that we would have to wait six or eight hours, the captain's wife came up from her retreat in the cabin and we stood together looking at the mangrove swamp. Inevitable maledictions were uttered as we watched the tide go down and the mud come shining to the surface in glistening purples and greens in early morning sun-light.

Eight hours' wait during the principal heat of the day! The place was not devoid of charm, for mud has its own kind of beauty. As the water drew back, I watched the bubbles pushing through the slime and the creatures that wriggled in the tiny creeks among the mangroves invading the water. Beyond the mangroves were screw-pines and dark-leaved bushes in tropical confusion.

A small jetty jutted out from the shore, which might indicate the near presence of a Fijian village. Our engineer, who had come perspiring from the little den in which he tended his engine, gave several piercing shouts, and a native appeared, walked down the jetty, and descended into a small boat that still floated in the retreating water. He paddled alongside, and all except the captain and his wife squeezed into the overladen boat. We made our way to the village, a mere cluster of leaf-built huts amid the surround-ing jungle. "Nothing much to do in a place like this," remarked the engineer, "but they don't mind; they are a lazy lot."

I strolled into the surrounding jungle, but was soon oppressed by the weight of fecundating vegetation. I came back to the jetty, and sat down in the shelter of dark mangrove leaves. Mangroves in their usual tangle of branching stems and up-thrusting breath-ing roots offered a vision of multitudes of slimy stems. The crude vegetation that flourished in the brackish water reminded me of something immensely old and well-founded. The creatures living amongst it soon made themselves evident. In the forks of the muddy branches sat little climbing fish, whose round protuberant eyes, starting from their heads, gazed in eagerness to view this cosmos of upper air, so different from mud and water. Sometimes they slipped from their perches and flopped back on to the mud, sank and disappeared, or wriggled down to small runnels of water.

As well as the climbing fishes there were small mud crabs, greyish in colour with blue markings on legs and back. One of the claws was always much larger than the other, conspicuous in red and white. This enlarged claw was so out of proportion that it must be bent upwards over the back of the carapace in order that the small bearer of this monstrosity might find balance enough to walk. As an organ it appeared useless, too heavy and too big to wield.

When I first met these mud-frequenting crabs I thought that

perhaps the crab had had originally two equal claws and had lost one, and was now growing another, not yet grown to full size. But mangrove crabs in most localities have one large and one small claw. The small one is for use and the large claw for show, brightly coloured and over-developed, held proudly and awkwardly aloft.

As the river water came back and the tide rose, the air became a trifle cooler and I roused myself from participation with mud and tangled stems of mangroves, whose very roots had changed into breathing organs. At last I heard the engineer and his companions returning from the house of some Fijian acquaintance where they had been drinking kava. With them I went back to the steamer, still haunted by the sight of mud and faint sound of breaking bubbles and a pungent scent of prehistory. By sunset we should be afloat again, and able to proceed.

About three months later I returned to Suva by the same paddle-steamer. Again I stood beside the German captain on the bridge and looked around at the tropical vegetation. We passed the usual remarks that men make on meeting again. He was as unchanged as the mud-flats. After a little, our conversation halted, and, thinking of something to say, I enquired whether his wife was well.

"Ah, zee is died, ze poor woman," he said. Then more cheerfully added, "But I has anozer one in ze cabin."

At the far end of the Rewa river lies the island of Mbau. This is a place of bloody memories, cruel traditions and orgiastic cannibal feasts. The island with all its equipment for pillage and human sacrifice was a monument of cruelty. Here gluttony for human flesh reached unusual development. The cannibalism of Mbau was different from the eating of enemies on special occasions, or of relatives who had died a natural or accidental death, and whose bodies were honoured by being made part of their surviving kinsmen, their souls thus being given a partial immortality.

On first landing on Mbau I took my letter of introduction to the house of the chieftain, a tall, sardonic man with a heavy crop of black hair. He took my letter from me in a rather offhand way, and I was left in doubt as to how we would get on together. As he read he smiled, though a little sourly, and invited me into his house. His house was built in usual native fashion, but was considerably larger than others that I saw later, and different in that the interior was divided into several rooms. The material for house-building consisted entirely of the products of the coconut palm. The supports at the corners and at the gabled end were of stems, and the walls, which were about thirty inches thick, were made of the leaves of the palms packed tightly together. The great ridge pole in the middle was made of several beams and supported in two places. The floor, raised four feet from the earth level, was packed tight with palm leaves and the floor space was covered by mats, deftly woven and finished with the red feathers of parrots. My host did not on this occasion offer me the national drink of yangona but suggested a whisky and water. Thus far sophistication had come, but I felt he was more deeply savage than any of my earlier companions among the Australian aborigines.

I was his guest for four nights. With a correct but cold courtesy, he showed me the sights. Mbau was a comparatively small island, but it was reputed to have provided, at the height of its fame, foothold for more than a thousand men and their families. These men had made themselves a terror to all the adjoining territory. They grew little food themselves, but extracted tribute from the nearby coast villages, raiding far in their war-canoes, which were a great deal larger than those usually in use. These canoes were eighty feet long, and were manned by twenty paddlers. Special stone-built docks had been made to harbour them. These were still in place at the time of my visit, though the war-canoes were but broken skeletons. At the launching of these craft, captives were laid bound on their backs, head to foot, their sides touching. Their bodies formed a living pavement from the building-site to the sea. The heavy keels were dragged over, leaving a trail of dead and dying. Once launched, the war-canoes with their pirate crews spread terror wherever they went. As soon as any village craft with man or woman or family party was sighted, it was chased and overtaken. A boat manned by twenty paddles could outpace any smaller canoe. The captives were not killed immediately, but were bound and carried back to Mbau.

On a small rise of ground was set a phallic stone about four feet in height. Close to the stone was the ruin of a large temple, and near by, a line of stone ovens built into the earth. The victims were dragged one by one to this spot, and there, when their captors had gathered round, their bonds were loosed. If they could dodge a way to the temple and win its sanctuary, their lives would be spared. The chance was small, and the practice was not devised in any spirit of fair play. When man or girl was captured for this second time, they were swung against the stone till their skulls cracked. The dead bodies were piled in a heap under a tree, which I saw still standing. The heap, on some occasions, touched a branch eight feet from the ground. Women, and especially young women, were valued most for their meat; their flesh offered the tenderest eating, particularly the inside of the thighs.

My host dwelt with some relish on this subject, and I guessed that he, in earlier years, had enjoyed human flesh. I asked whether the twenty paddlers of a war-canoe could eat so much as could be piled under the tree. They could eat a good deal, he said, but not always all. They ate the tenderest bits from the younger bodies. What was not eaten was thrown into the sea.

The body was cooked whole, and that I might appreciate how it was done, my host had a young pig killed and prepared in the way that a man or woman might have been prepared in the old days before a British warship sailed into Suva harbour. This was not pleasant to witness. The pig began screaming, as pigs always do when death is near. It was clubbed on the head, but not thoroughly, then dragged close to the heated oven from which embers had been scraped out. During the singeing it revived and began to scream again, much to the amusement of the cooks. After another knock on the head it was disembowelled, and the belly cavity lined with banana leaves and then filled with hot stones. The body was then wrapped in layers of banana leaves, and placed in the oven. After several hours of gently cooking in its own juice the pig was ready for the finishing ritual. It was taken from the black and charred layers of leaves, and its face was shaved and painted in bright colours. The roasted pig took on a human look, and it was not difficult to imagine a well-cooked man or girl. The creature was served whole. My host severed the limbs and cut out the best morsels. The Fijians are master cooks, and their method of leaf-cooking cannot be excelled. The pig was made to take a sitting posture in imitation of the human victims. Good as it tasted, I was assured that "long-pig" tasted better.

Not only were the less ferocious neighbours of Mbau murdered for food, or sacrificed under the keels of war-canoes, but when the great temple was built, twenty living men were buried under each of the corner uprights. Part of the temple was at that time still standing, though part had already fallen into ruin. It was the largest native building I was to see in Fiji.

The phallic stone against which so many skulls had been broken had been set up in a Christian church to serve as a font. The British warships cruising among the islands reminded the population that the old customs were no more, and that now a new era of peace and goodwill had come among men. Yet I had a strong feeling, while on Mbau, that the reminder was necessary, and that though the Fijians were so correct in manner, I might, had it not been for those reassuring wisps of smoke on the horizon, have been cooked and eaten.

Amongst the Australian aborigines I had no such uneasy feeling. They were more primitive, and far less polite, but with them I had felt secure, however far I was from European influence. Although the aborigines of Australia were cruel in their way, they were not deliberately cruel. They would break the legs of any captured animal so that it might not run away, and would remain fresh against the time that they wanted to kill it. This was necessity, since they had no refrigerators. The Fijians took delight in killing. While I was on Mbau a dog was hunted, just an ordinary stray dog that nobody seemed to want. It was chased with sticks and stones for a considerable time, and when it at last took refuge in the sea men swam after it and drowned it. Another sign of native cruelty, which was largely pandered to by the European community, were shooting booths common in the towns. A cock or a hen was tied by the leg and natives paid a penny a shot with air-gun slugs at the unfortunate animal. I have seen cocks with both eyes shot out. The man who finally killed the bird had it to eat. The money collected from these shooting booths went to the building or restoration of the magnificent Roman Catholic cathedral in Suva. This seemed shocking to some of the Europeans, but it might be considered a natural adaptation to the way of the country.

I spent the inside of a week on the island of Mbau, wandering for most of the time free from the attentions of my host, and trying to understand this centre of piracy. I tried to imagine those thousand warrior supermen who were so justly and universally feared, and whose war-canoes ventured even so far as the northern shores of Vanua Levu. At night I slept on a Fijian couch wrapped in a roll of tapa. I got something of the feeling of the place, and as I did so became increasingly restless and anxious to move away.

My host offered to take me in his motor launch to Levuka, that had once been the capital of the islands. It was from here that I was to make an expedition into less sophisticated parts. He was going across in any case, and would take me with him. The day before I was to go I asked him to give me back my letter of introduction. He handed it to me with his impersonal and distant smile. I would have liked to ask him to interpret the writing, but something held me back. This man, who could speak English so well, had formed his own opinion of the contents of the letter, whatever this might be. He had also, no doubt, summed me up as an inexperienced young man. I did not want to give him an opportunity to expose me further.

On the night before my departure I knew that the time of offering gifts had come. I did not know what I should offer, for he was no doubt a rich and influential man. In some uneasiness I offered him a very good English knife, containing several gadgets as well as two blades. He accepted it without showing any sign, yet his acceptance was perfectly courteous. He gave me as a parting gift a large and magnificent roll of tapa which stood me in good stead as a blanket on cold nights.

As the boat charged through the waves on its way to Levuka I was glad to be leaving the blood-tainted atmosphere of Mbau. The relics of more savage days still held their ancient *mana*. Having partaken with undisguised satisfaction of the painted pig, so human in appearance, I felt that I myself was almost a cannibal.

On the landing-stage at Levuka I said a final farewell to my host, and made my way to the local hotel, and thence to the magistrate who was to help me to find a boat and crew for my expedition to the island of Moturiki. He received my note of introduction and then glanced through the letter I had for the local chiefs, the "passport" letter. Here, I thought, was the man who would translate. Smiling, he shook his head. Let it speak for itself. He asked how the chieftain of Mbau had received it. Had I enjoyed my stay there? I told him I had seen many interesting monuments of past times. He replied that the villages on Moturiki were very different.

I enjoyed the two days' wait at Levuka, wandering about the town and port, watching the people. The young native men had their thick hair brushed straight up; some had it whitened with lime. The native policemen were naked to the waist, but wore dark blue sarongs fastened with a belt of coconut fibres. Each carried a formidable club with a bifurcated end. The native girls were also naked to the waist; their hair was much shorter than the men's and tightly curled to their heads. Many of the Levuka natives could talk English. During this time I did my best to study Fijian vocabulary, and I learnt several phrases by heart. This proved fortunate, for on meeting my crew I found that none could speak one word of English. The policeman knew a few English phrases, about as many as I knew of Fijian.

The friendly magistrate took me to the wharf and introduced me to my crew of convicts, six lusty young men all convicted by missionary law of the venal sin of fornication. They showed no sign of being under constraint, and appeared happy and laughing at the prospect of a pleasant journey amongst the inland waters of the lagoon.

I had with me two knapsacks, my beating tray and butterfly net, and a great many collecting boxes. These were stowed under the stern seats of what had once been an old whaler, now rigged to carry six oars. The policeman stood in the stern with a steering paddle. I sat beside him, and we pushed off into a slightly choppy sea. Soon we entered the strait that lay between Moturiki on our left and Ovalau on the right. The Fijian lads rowed well, and as I had considered myself a bit of a "wet-bob" I determined to take a place with an oar before we had finished our journey. For this first stretch I would be a spectator, and certainly had plenty to look at. We had not started till early afternoon, and when we entered the lagoon evening was drawing on. While we were in the comparatively open sea, rounding the shore of Ovalau, my convicts sang in unison as they struck the wave furrows, but when we reached still water they stopped as they rested on their oars. We listened to the cries of sea-birds mingling with those of others from the jungle uplands on either side. After a pause we paddled gently on. These offenders, had they wished, could easily have overcome the policeman, and have thrown both him and me into the lagoon. But they all seemed on the easiest of terms. The wages that I was to pay were six dried tobacco leaves a day for the policeman, and for the convicts only one each. I decided to double this quota, since the bunches of dried leaves cost only one and sixpence a pound.

To attempt to describe the corals that flourished in the shallow waters of the lagoon would be wasted effort. I looked down through a glass-bottomed bucket, thus avoiding the ripple, and saw many brilliant creatures and plants of a tropic sea. The coral plants were different from those of the reefs, not built to withstand the buffeting of waves, but delicately branched. Their living polyps, which grew like flowers on their stems, were of iridescent blue, purple and green. Among them were dark brown, sharply spiked echinoderms. More rarely seen were fantastically shaped sea slugs, and sluggish holothurians that lay like black and pimply sausages inert on this many-coloured carpet. There were brightly tinted fish, all small in size, maintaining position with a mere ripple of fins.

I was divided between looking at the sea floor and the volcanic hills on either side as they took the evening light. Across the jagged line of hilltops flew a flock of pale pink miniature herons. The scene was all, and more than all, I had expected; it overcame the suspense of not knowing what was to be my destination, or how I would be able to meet these unknown villagers.

Half an hour after sundown, when darkness was swiftly gathering, we turned into the mouth of a small river. We rowed between coconut plantations, and entered a tunnel where tropical foliage met in an arch. The water was black and smooth, the only sound the dipping of our oars.

At a small pier we disembarked, and beside my policeman I followed the path. On the outskirts of the village he took my letter and told me to wait. He and his crew went on, leaving me alone to look around into the tree stems where huge platycerium ferns were outlined against the sky, like prehistoric monsters that had climbed and stuck there.

It was a long wait: a poor reception, I thought, auguring no good. It proved to be the prelude to an embarrassingly grand one.

My letter had produced an astonishing effect. A family had been turned out of one of the houses. This was to be mine during my stay. After a long time two young men approached, one carrying a torch blazing at the end with sticky resin. Both had pale yellow hair-dressings. They squatted on their heels, and he who did not hold a torch, clapped his hands and uttered "Wah! Wah! Wah!", as though to indicate "Welcome, thou great one!"

I did not know how to respond adequately, but said, as confidently as I could, "Vanarka, vanarka. Eo sar vanarka," a stock phrase which seemed to fit most occasions. Recovering in a single bound to upright position, my guides led me to the village. I was taken to the chief's house where a number of men were gathered. Soon we were all seated for the drinking of yangona. Yangona is a native root, which the English government had decreed must no longer be prepared by the chewing of the root by the village maidens. It was at this time made by rubbing the root on a rough stone. The product of the rubbing was then swished round in a large bowl by loofahs. When a sufficient rinsing had been given, a coconut shell full of the drink was handed to the chief. He quaffed it, and flinging it down into the middle of the room, exclaimed "Wah! Wah!" and then clapped his hands. A nutful was then handed to me by a young man squatting on his heels. I followed the example of the chief, clapped my hands, and exclaimed "Wah! Wah!" The nut was refilled and handed round in sequence to each of the men present.

The drink to my uninitiated palate tasted rather like brown paper. During my visit to the islands I grew to value it highly. It had no obvious intoxicating effect, but exercised a gentle influence, without which I would have found it hard to sustain the many long ceremonial and other dances that I was obliged to attend. It had no ill effects.

My house was a beautiful building about sixty feet long by twenty feet wide. There were doors on each side so that one could always find a draught to sit in. The floor, raised three feet from earth-level, was covered with mats. The walls were built of leaves tightly packed as were those of the houses on Mbau. Across one end, raised about three feet, was a shelf six feet deep. It extended the whole width of the house. There was no other furniture. On this shelf I was to sleep in solitary glory, while quite a number of natives slept on the floor. I soon found that whatever privileges I was to be given, privacy was not to be one of them. Indeed throughout all my stay in these remote villages I was seldom alone.

After the yangona drinking, food was brought in and heaped in a pile thirty inches high on a central mat. Each article of food was wrapped in fresh banana leaves. I had never seen such a dinner. There were roasted chicken, fish and crayfish, yams and bread-fruit, and delicious green coconuts to drink. There were pawpaws and grenadillas, bananas both cooked and raw. Two Fijian youths had been instructed to be my personal attendants. If I did not eat what they considered the best bits, they would pick out the morsels and present them to my lips. My failing, which soon

Fijian native dancers (*above*)
Village of coconut palms in Fiji (*below*)

Native Fijian lugger, similar to the one in which the author travelled to Koro

Reef coral at low tide in Fiji

became too evident, was that I could not eat enough to compare with the national standard, and what troubled me was that my hosts refused to eat any of this glorious meal until I had finished. They then fell to and showed what eating really could be. The dislodged family were appointed as my particular hosts. I began to guess at the contents of the letter. I had been introduced as a great chief from Cambridge, or more probably *the* great chief, as I heard the word "Cambridge" frequently mentioned in the speeches that were made, or the songs that were improvised.

At last when all food was cleared away, and after a welcoming dance by some girls in sitting posture, decked in sweet-scented herbs, I was allowed to stretch out on my ample bed.

Part of the difficulty of living in a Fijian village was that I knew only half a dozen phrases of the language. The villagers knew no English, since the missionary, their only contact, spoke Fijian. We could smile at one another and gesticulate. They talked their language, and I talked mine. Laughter is a common language and the Fijians laughed a great deal. When I emerged from my house in the morning, young people took charge of me, the boys taking me to bathe where water from a brook was conveyed along bamboo pipes to the height convenient for a shower. After the bath we oiled ourselves with pale green coconut oil that smelt delicious. On the way from the baths, girls waited, some of them presenting me with hibiscus flowers to put behind my ears, others with streamers of European-type toilet paper, doubtless the property of the missionary. I was conducted to a rickety little pier that jutted some fifty feet into the sea. This, as far as I can remember the name, was *lillelilvalee*, one of the "conveniences" used by both sexes. To say I was embarrassed is putting it mildly. There was no doubt in their unsophisticated minds that here I was expected to do my morning duty. My first concern was to walk along those narrow planks without falling into the sea. Well, if this was the custom of the country, I was "for it". I must endure the presence of an expectant crowd. The shoal of small fish in the water below were well acquainted with the *lillelilvalee*, and came for their morning meal.

I was soon to find that three or four visits to the shower were the order of every day. The Fijians are a cleanly people; their brown skins shone like silk in sunlight, and the constant rubbing with the sweet-scented oil gave an attractive odour. For occupation, both old and young were engaged in laughing, idling, swimming and fishing, though some of the more elderly were at work on the serious occupations of mat-making, tapa-beating, and cooking. No organized form of agriculture was undertaken in the village. There was no need, since many vegetable foods grew wild in the jungle: many kinds of banana, yams, ndalo-root that had leaves like an arum lily, pawpaws and bread-fruit to name but a few. Coconut palms were a native growth, grouped in plantations near the shore. A few nuts were planted every year, protected from the jungle growth and from a species of ants that attacked them. From the coconut came both flesh and drink. and no drink could be nicer than the juice yielded by the unripe nut. The flesh could be prepared in many attractive ways; that of the young nuts was often whipped into a delicious cream.

A few pigs ran semi-wild in a large enclosure, grubbing for their own food. Chickens ran loose; they were killed and cooked while yet warm, wrapped in banana leaves. Fishing was the chief activity of the younger men. Many kinds were speared, and many were trapped in reed fences which were built out into the sea, and then curved back on themselves in an open helix-spiral. The trap was simple; fish swam in with the rising tide, were held in the spiral curve, and when the water withdrew, were caught by hand in the shallows. There was a small thick-fleshed sole that lay concealed in the coral sand, and many varieties of free-swimming fish. A more exciting way of fishing was by torchlight on the edge of the reef. Holding torches near the water, we waited until the inquisitive ones rose to look at the light. They could then be speared. Although not so skilled as the natives at this sport, I could hold my own. Fresh-water species of fish were in brooks and small rivers, and crayfish, scampi, I think, that looked like large prawns. These were exceedingly good to eat, both cooked and raw. There was one species of fish that the natives ate alive, biting off the head and then eating down to the tail. In the lagoon were crabs and holothurians. These latter were exported in large numbers by visiting Chinese fishermen, who first dried them in the sun; they had a strong penetrating smell. There were also sea-worms that appeared in great quantities at certain phases of the moon. They were much valued, and made into a thick soup. There were oysters, but not so sweet-tasting as the smaller specimens from Bernier Island. There was always abundance of delicious food that could be got with very little trouble. Why, indeed, should people so happily placed need to work? Protected by the government, they kept near to the original paradise. It had at one time been broken by raids of the cannibal tribes from Mbau, but those raids were forgotten. No wars or rumours of wars had yet been heard on those silver and gold-sanded beaches, fringed with coconut palms.

Out from the village went many paths. My two body-servants followed me, carrying the collecting apparatus. What they must have thought of my activities I never guessed. But they treated this eccentric chief from Cambridge with unfailing toleration, and soon entered into my peculiar form of madness, being quick to collect beetles, butterflies, stick-insects and mantis.

My concern was how to preserve my collections, which soon grew to large dimensions. Had I not read Charles Waterton's *Wanderings In South America*, I would not have brought my collections back, for there were small red ants that penetrated everywhere and ate all they could set jaws to, including the collecting papers in which I preserved butterflies. Waterton recommended a mixture of water and spirit, with the right addition of mercuric chloride. This defied all insect-eatings, even those of the minute ants which could crawl through the smallest cracks.

The interior of the island was rough volcanic rock, but where the tufa was decaying, a rich vegetation flourished, one plant crowding upon another and all interlaced with the rough lianas of creepers. To get through this would have been impossible but for the native paths leading to many delectable spots with tall grasses and flowering herbs.

Storms were frequent, short and violent. Sheets of rain poured, drenching and cold, but soon the sun was shining again, drawing up warm, earth-smelling vapours to make clouds for the next rain storm. A light shirt, that would soon be dry, was the best garment for such a climate. If the storm was unusually long and the rain too chilling, I followed the example of my companions, wading into the sea which was always warmer than the rain.

The bathing was wonderful; my well-oiled body was soon as dark as the Fijians, indeed darker than some. When I returned to England and met R. C. Trevelyan, who later became a close friend, we went to swim together in a pond near Dorking. He thought I was a coloured man.

On most days I sat in my doorway either reading or writing. To write did not seem so provocative of wonder as did reading. The natives could not imagine what I was up to. I happened to have with me a second-hand copy of stories by Henry James that I had picked up in Sydney. These ultra-sophisticated tales, which the assurance of their author had named *The Better Sort*, seemed appropriate reading in this remote village, whose culture dated back to the late neolithic age. While I read, passing natives would pause and watch in respectful curiosity, silent and absorbed. Whenever I turned a page he would give a gently breathed "Wah! Wah!" Having gazed his fill and watched the turning of several pages, he would move on, and after a time some other man or woman would come up and repeat this little comedy. I could not guess what the turning of the pages might mean for the silent watcher.

My most solitary times were with my two attendants in jungle paths or open glades, or when swimming in the sea. One event raised me high in their estimation. I had with me a small apparatus for the cure of snake-bite, a boxwood cylinder with a small knife in one end and some crystals of permanganate of potash in the other. While wading on the beach one of the men trod on a stinging fish. He was convulsed in agony, and could not contain his screams. Fortunately my little cylinder was handy. I stabbed the place and pushed into the wound a crystal of permanganate. The result was magical—the pain at once subsided, and screams turned to a laugh. The permanganate had oxidized the poisonous alkaloid. I was from then on not only a great chief from Cambridge but a medicine man of high efficiency. Better was to follow, for when Sunday came I was to prove myself a successful preacher.

Since the advent of the missionary the days of the week were kept, and it was conveyed to me that on the Sunday my presence was expected in the church where the minister preached on his half-yearly visits. The Christian faith had divided the islands between Roman Catholics and Wesleyans, and this village happened to be Wesleyan. The church was built on the same plan as the old-time heathen temple, but was smaller and far less pretentious. It was a picturesque building of compressed and tightly bound coconut leaves, its interior cool and spacious, its floor of leaves covered with woven mats, the furniture a solitary European chair. To this chair I was led, and told by signs to sit on it. The congregation, both men and women, settled themselves on the floor. After a hymn, sung in the sitting position but with a good deal of arm swaying, one of the elders sprang to his feet, and addressed the meeting with the most spirited speech, his words pouring out in an unchecked stream. I guessed that he was talking chiefly to me, and of me, since he often pointed in my direction and the word "Cambridge" recurred frequently. Then followed longer hymns, sung with great gusto, with swaying from the hips and flinging out of arms.

As soon as the first speaker sat down, another took his place—another speech, another singing interval, and so on till several men had had their say. They were enjoying it thoroughly, though I was beginning to wonder how long it would last. I had never before sat so long in church. Although this worship was far more animated than any other I had attended, I was beginning to get bored, and wishing I could get away for a dip in the sea.

Two men came up to me and gently touched my arms, intimating that I should get up and address the meeting. For at least three long seconds I was completely flummoxed. How could I possibly make any sort of showing after the streams of rhetoric that had flowed from the previous speakers?

An inspiration came to me—I realized that I knew a great many lines of English poetry. I started on George Meredith's "Woods of Westermain" without fear of over-emphasis: "Enter these enchanted Woods, you who dare." I recited most of it, a long poem, then switched to parts of Shelley's "Prometheus Un-bound", followed by Keats' "Ode to Psyche". Here I paused, but seeing the mood of my audience swayed by this uninhibited flow of words, I thought of Vachel Lindsay's "Congo", of which I knew the closing lines:

> Death is an Elephant,
> Torch-eyed and horrible,
> Foam-flanked and terrible.
> *Boom*, Steal the pygmies,
> *Boom*, Kill the Arabs,
> *Boom*, Kill the white men.
> Hoo, Hoo, Hoo.

> Listen to the yell of Leopold's ghost
> Burning in Hell for his hand-maimed host.
> Hear how the demons chuckle and yell

Cutting his hands off, down in Hell.
Listen to the creepy proclamation
Blown through the lairs of the forest-nation,
Blown past the white ants' hill of clay,
Blown past the marsh where the butterflies play:—

> "Be careful what you do,
> Or Mumbo-Jumbo, God of the Congo,
> And all of the other
> Gods of the Congo,
> Mumbo-Jumbo will hoo-doo you.
> Mumbo-Jumbo will hoo-doo you."

The last lines had accents heavy and light and the final line was whispered.

The effect on my audience was astonishing. They leapt to their feet, crying "Wah! Wah! Wah! Vanarka! Vanarka!" and clapped hands in unison. I had not expected such acclamation and felt a spasm of shame. But in the circumstances I had to do something. "Vanarka! Vanarka!" they repeated, which I understood to mean "Encore!"

I sat down abashed. What was I doing playing on the emotions of these good people? At least I must calm them before we went down to the cleansing waters of the sea, to swim together as ordinary men. But what could I do since I could not directly communicate?

They continued to clap their hands and say "Wah! Wah!" Swinburne might sound a bit insipid after the Devils of the Congo, but it was the best I could think of. I was so much influenced by the swaying gestures of my audience and the cadence of their reiterated incantations that I almost sang "The Forsaken Garden". It was approved but not encored. They had not understood a word, but the rhythm was already in their hearts. In gentler mood we went down to the sea and from thence to a good dinner. I wondered what the missionary would be told on his next visit.

Life was so pleasant at that village that I had no inclination to rove further. Why leave paradise for uncertainty? My convicts also seemed content. Each day they were decked in wreaths by village maidens, and since no missionary was present, I thought it probable they were adding to their sentences. This was not my affair, and my policeman was happily engaged in his own amorous adventures. Why trouble a garden into which no serpent had offered the knowledge of good and evil? The reef and all its charm was there for discovery, a delight to any biologist. At low tide there were pools with plants and animals, fresh from the source of creation. On the reefs were fresh, lovely ponds, shallow and deep, each a little world in itself. Many hours I spent picking up discarded shells of creatures that once had lived—opercula, like cat's eyes, and opals, that had once been carried on the tails of sea snails. I collected bags full of beautiful shells, some as large as the pearl oyster, some so small and delicate that they could be blown away by any passing zephyr. There were blue-tinted shells of a miniature nautilus that once sailed serene on the Pacific waves—a thing easily destroyed, yet surviving. In contrast there were enormous shells of living clams. These were a danger, for if a careless foot were placed in them, they would close and hold tight. Many a man had been drowned in their grip. These clam shells, dead or alive, were regarded by the natives with religious awe. They were "women-shells", resembling those parts most important to the primitive mind.

After my sermon in the church there was a good deal of conversation in which both men and women took part. I gathered that some sort of celebration was being planned, and it was intimated that I should witness a women's dance inside my house, and that later in the cool of the evening the men, as warriors of the tribe, would do a war dance.

At the appointed time most of the population of the village squeezed themselves into my house. Those privileged among them sat on the raised bed beside me. The ceremony started with drinking yangona. A troupe of girls entered, swathed about in sweet-smelling herbs; they seated themselves just under the raised dais and began to sing, swaying from the hips and dancing with rhythmical movements of arms and hands. This would have been fine if it had not gone on for so exceedingly long. The atmosphere was heavily charged with the odour of bruised leaves, human sweat and coconut oil. Every now and then there was a pause, and all would clap in unison, exclaiming "Vanarka! Vanarka!" Yangona was handed round in cups of coconut shells. For this I was grateful for its numbing effect made it possible to endure more and yet more of the singing.

Meal-time came at last, preceded by a dip in the sea. Refreshed and replete we all had a pause and a sleep. In the afternoon the stage was set for the dance of the warriors. Some of the men were painted in red, black and ochre, and all had war-clubs and spears. The missionary's chair from the church had been brought out for me to sit on. These dances did not last for so long as the women's dances, though they were performed with great zest. Spears were hurled over my head, and finally they all rushed upon me with raised clubs and shouted war-cries.

I clapped my hands and kept my seat. Shouts and a great deal of talk followed, more yangona drinking, and again to the sea. Then, at last, to bed.

After a week spent in exploring the jungle paths, wading in the lagoon and coral pools, I ordered my policeman to gather his crew for an expedition to the outer reef of Moturiki. We rowed in the open sea round the southern shore of the island. The fringing reef was not far from the land, and quiet water lay between them. The tide was ebbing, and we could walk over the hard and flattened surface of rock. I needed rope-soled shoes to provide a sure foothold, though the natives' feet were sufficiently hardened. The waves of the Pacific broke gently on outermost growths of coral, and here the coral animals were in the most favourable situation. In the reef were many channels, some broad, some narrow. Sea water rushed to meet the ebbing tide.

The coral shelf that had fringed the west coast of Bernier Island was my first experience of massive coral. There the breakers of the Indian Ocean had been a wonder as they crashed on the step of the reef; here the slow, enormous swell of the Pacific as it spent itself conveyed a greater experience. Here I was alone, in the midst of the sea, with lagoon behind and the ocean in front—alive in the midst of many waters! My convict crew had dispersed in search of crayfish in the recesses of the swirling clefts. I was knee-deep in warmth alive with creatures, those that I could see and those I could not, floating invisible and transparent. Soft airs carried the indescribable scent of ocean.

As the tide ebbed I picked up shells of molluscs that had died and left their tokens. There were large cowrie shells from two or three inches long that had been wholly enclosed while alive in the soft flesh of the animals that during the years had fashioned them.

Since they had not been in contact with the outer world, they had a shining glaze tinted with patterns of pink, brown and purple. Their mouths, tinted and ribbed, led into cavities, now empty and secret, which had once guarded the vital organs.

I had no means of finding out how the Fijians had arranged their marriages before the coming of the missionaries, but I learned from an old sailor that I met on the beach at Suva how the problems of old age were solved so far as women were concerned. At the appointed time, when their ailments were becoming a nuisance or they happened to talk too much, they were buried alive with only their heads remaining above the earth. He had seen women buried in this manner with heads protruding from their graves. They accepted their fate with courage, saluting him as he passed: "Vanarka, vanarka." He was sorry but could do nothing, only feeling relief when the heads had fallen on one side, no longer able to answer his greeting. Old men suffered no such curtailment.

Yet they had diseases, even in the happy villages on Moturiki. There was scale-skin, produced by prolonged drinking of yangona; there was bung-eye, and most noticeable and shocking, elephantiasis, a disease caused by filarian worm that entered the bloodstream with the bite of a mosquito. Probably everyone, white or native, who lived for many months in Fiji, was infected. The disease, however, was slow to assume the elephantine growths of arms and legs. Usually only one limb was elephantine in growth, but sometimes the disease had gone further. I remember being horror-struck by one unfortunate who was compelled to crawl around. Both legs were swollen so greatly that scrotum and penis were altogether enveloped in hillocks of flesh, only a small hole remaining for a flow of urine. The picture of this man, who seemed wonderfully cheerful in the circumstances, haunted me for many days.

No earthly paradise is as perfect as it may first appear. Disease, hurricanes and cold, drenching rains, mosquitoes, and stinging fish, stinging medusae and sharks, all bring one back to earthly reality. Cannibal pirates, missionaries, measles, syphilis and influenza cloud the pristine innocence.

I made my final passage to the lagoon early one morning. Preparations had been made and farewells spoken. I had given knives, tobacco and pipes to the men, kerchiefs and beads to the girls. Most of the village turned out to say goodbye. We were all presented with garlands. My collecting apparatus was carried by my body-servants, and the boat was launched while a song (or was it a hymn?) was sung. As we glided down the river and came to the yellow reed fishing-traps I thought of the letters I hoped to find at the Poste Restante at Suva.

The letters were there. Some reproached me for not taking up the post that I had obtained through the Appointments Board at Cambridge, which had been considered so fortunate and safe. I stuffed them in my pocket, and went to a tailor's shop kept by an Indian, and ordered two new tussore silk suits. This sounds, in modern values, an extravagant outlay, but in Fiji silk suits could be made to measure at that time for thirty shillings. My intention was to present myself at the house of the Lord Chief Justice, and the short skirts that I had worn on Moturiki were not suitable.

My letter of introduction, and the new suit, worked the white man's magic, and I was invited to stay for an unspecified time. My memories of this visit, though not so vivid as those of native life, are of a great kindness, and admission into the charmed circle of "Government House". Ghosts from Trinity College, Cambridge, helped me, and I began to feel myself almost an English gentleman again. It was a pleasant novelty to sit at table with knife and fork, and not to squat on the ground and eat with my fingers, or more probably from the fingers of my attentive servant. Of the people I met I have memories of only two. The Lord Chief Justice himself was all that an English host could be. He was much liked and, in his kindness, offered to take me with him on an an official trip to the Windward Islands. This was to be a journey of indeterminate length, and I did not feel I could for so long commit myself. I would have liked to visit those coral atolls, but I was warned that the small government steamer was notorious for both rolling and pitching. I pictured myself terribly sea-sick.

The other man that stays in my memory was a pure-blooded negro. He was a doctor; he spoke perfect English and, to my surprise, was admitted without any question into the upper strata of society. He was married to an exceptionally fair and, I thought, lovely English girl. They had two infant children that took their colour more from their mother than their father. Dr. Lynch was popular with everyone, and it may have been his exceptional abilities that had overcome the colour-bar.

I was never quite at ease in this society but cherished an inward guilt, feeling that my place was elsewhere. My real place was "the Beach", where all kinds of rag, tag and bobtail gathered. These were men who had either prospered or failed in various jobs, owners of sailing cutters full of dried coconuts, pearl-shells and sethi. They had lived in very smelly boats, or had combed the coral beaches of neighbouring islands, collecting bêche-de-mer to dry in the sun and ship to China, or perhaps were, or had been, engaged in pearling, or were under contract to empty earth-privies in the suburbs.

There was a man called George Prothero, who had knocked around the South Seas—a Conrad character who was full of stories. His present job was looking for sethi and the shells of pearl oysters. He invited me to go for a short trip, which I accepted gladly. His boat was a lugger of some fifteen tons, and it smelt remarkably highly of earlier catches. We had two native divers with us, and we set out for a bank some twenty miles distant.

While the boat was in motion the smell was not bad so long as I could sit in the wind. We dropped anchor in a sheltered cove, and the divers began their work which they carried on without diving apparatus. They had big knives to cut the oysters free, and bags to put them in. There was a weighted ladder hung over the side, and on this, when they could hold their breath no longer, they climbed back with their burden. The shells, from four to eight inches across, were laid on the deck, where in scorching sunlight the living contents would soon open in their death gasps. When a sufficient number had been brought up we all turned to with knives to scrape the flesh from the shells, feeling, as we did so, for the possibility of a pearl being contained therein. We came on several, but nothing of particular value, as these pearls were of odd shapes. Most of the flesh was thrown back into the sea, though a small portion was retained to be eaten. The shells were packed in bundles. All kinds of living organisms clung to the outer sides —small sponges, serpular worms, anemones and countless small creatures. These, together with the flesh fragments that had not been scraped clear of the shells, soon began to decompose, producing the atrocious stink in which we lived and worked. Strange, I thought, to have landed myself into such a fishy odour when I might have had my feet under a table and be eating like an English gentleman.

The shells, rather than the chance of odd pearls, were the object of our work. At that time they were worth about two hundred pounds a ton, and from them were made all kinds of small objects like pearl buttons and studs. For ten days we sweltered in tropical heat, relieved by swimming in those clear and beautiful seas. I tried my hand at diving for shell, but found I could not hold my breath long enough. This was long before the days of Captain Cousteau with frog-feet and breathing apparatus. Sometimes we went ashore and loafed and fed. I was always glad to get away from the stench.

While on this short expedition, George told me of the island of Koro in the Koro Sea. If I was interested in magic I should not miss going there. From a high cliff on that island, turtles were called to come up and show themselves. It was a sight worth seeing. George said that he could put me in the way of a native seaman who went over regularly. And how would I get back? There were boats going and coming all the time as the wind changed, he said.

Most of the time I slept ashore, wrapping myself up in a roll of tapa on the coral sand. Many armies of crabs came to find out what I was. I had to wrap my head up to prevent my ears being sampled. Had I been dead, they would no doubt have had fine meals. Fortunately, they kept their hours and did not come out of their holes till dark.

The late afternoons and evenings were the times I liked best; the wind that blew during the day dropped suddenly and, as light began to fade, colours became more intense. In the pause between day and night I would sometimes feel strangely suspended between the present and my remembered life in Europe. Was this wandering about the southern seas merely an idle luxury? Certainly I was not spending much money, for everywhere hospitality was offered, whether in the Lord Chief Justice's house, in a Fijian village, or in a stinking old pearl-lugger.

George, true to his word, introduced me to a native boat-owner who would take me for the modest sum of ten shillings to the distant island of Koro.

The island of Koro lies about sixty miles northwest of Ovalau. At Levuka I was introduced to the Fijian family who were to give me passage in their ten-ton cutter. Intending but a short visit, I took only a knapsack.

I stepped aboard about midnight, and lay on the deck watching the mast-head make patterns among the stars. I dozed, then slept, and woke when we were hoisting sail. Day was dawning, a light breeze came off the land. With the rising sun, the wind stiffened. The boat was crowded with natives. There was no chance, even if I wanted to, of penetrating to the cabin. I took up my position in the bows and for most of the way enjoyed the voyage enormously. Although I was soon wet with spray, this was an advantage in warm air. By the time the sun rose we were well out to sea, with numberless blue hilly island peaks spotting the horizon to westward. Midway on our passage my companions offered a variety of foods—cooked yams and ndalo, bananas and oranges. These were all included in the ten shillings for my fare. We made a quick passage with a marching wind on our beam and by afternoon I was put ashore on a small pier at a place called Matana. This was the private landing of the plantation owner, a man called Peterson.

There was no one on the jetty when I arrived, so I shouldered my knapsack and walked through the coconut plantation towards a pleasant-looking bungalow perched on a rise above the flat land of the plantation. Here I encountered a native woman who had several small children. I told her I had come to stay with Mr. Peterson and would she prepare me an evening meal. This request she took as a matter of course. Two of the small boys were told to catch a chicken. Its neck was broken, its feathers plucked, and she began to cook it in the native fashion. She was a pleasant woman and could, I was glad to find, speak a little English.

Having learned something of the ways of the land I did not hesitate to enter the house. In the sitting-room were deck chairs and a good many out-of-date English magazines, showing signs of being much read. Since Peterson made no sign of returning, she served me my meal alone. She was not a wife but a cook-housekeeper who shared the man's bed. The bird was excellent, served with coconut cream, ndalo, small red bananas and paw-paws.

In the late evening the planter turned up, and was delighted to find a guest. He said I could stay as long as I liked—a week, a month, a year, the longer the better. As for payment, he would not hear of it. Everything he had was at my disposal. He told me he had not seen another white man for more than a month, when the lugger had come to take away his copra. I complimented him on his wife's cooking. He immediately said that he would send one of his native boys to catch fish for us, and he had a young porker that would come in most fortunately. Such hospitality over-whelmed me; guests were much valued on inaccessible islands, as they were very rare.

During the first day at Matana, while my host was away at the drying mats, I explored the plantation and the beach. This plantation was larger than most, with hundreds of trees stretching along the coast; the beach was superb, with clear, warm water, white sands and innumerable shells and opercula scattered along the strand. Some were as small as the old-time threepenny bits, some as much as two inches across. These had been the back doors to close the houses of sea shells. They showed a great uniformity of colour, grey-blue shading to a dark pupil like cat's eyes. After a swim I went along the path through the plantation. Here and there natives were engaged in the skilled task of cutting the copra from the shells.

A stake pointed at each end had been driven into the soil, a couple of feet protruding above the surface. By banging the nut and its fibrous case hard against this spike, the nut was cracked open. This was not difficult, but getting the flesh out of the shell was a different matter. Three strokes of the knife should be sufficient for a practised hand; I found when I tried that I needed ten or twelve. The milk of the nut was wasted. From time to time a native collected the flesh on a hand truck and wheeled it off to be spread out on drying mats. The drying of the copra is not so easy as it might seem, for the island was subject to constant short bursts of heavy rain. Against these storms the copra had to be protected till it was judged dry enough to be stored in sheds, there to be collected by the visiting craft. In the process the delicious smell of the fresh nut changed to a pungent stench. The native oil was derived straight from the fresh nuts, but the commercial oil had to be purified.

After watching with admiration the quick turns that extracted the flesh from the nuts, I walked on through the plantation to the drying mats, which were made of reeds and lifted a suitable distance from the earth. Here I found Peterson at the auspicious moment when his wife arrived with an excellent meal. While we ate I told him of my wish to visit the cliff from whose height the turtles were called. It might be managed, he said, but the natives were not always obliging. I told him of my passport letter. He glanced at it, but although he could speak Fijian fluently, he could not read the missionary-made script. "I'll send one of my boys with it to Nathamaki. We can but try. Can't do any harm." He paused, then said, "If you want magic you've come to the right place."

"You believe in it?" I asked.

"I can't help it. The plantation is haunted. Not a native will come near after sundown. Even my missus won't go out. The tree-tops are full of devil-devils."

"Have you seen them?"

"I've taken good care not to, but I've heard them clear enough in the plantation, moving through the tree-tops."

"I did not hear anything odd last night," I said.

"They don't come every night, only on still nights."

At this point Peterson broke off and went back to his work. I strolled further along the strand, till I came to the village that supplied the men working on the plantation. It seemed a very ordinary village, I thought, neat, well-ordered and clean. Some women were beating tapa, the native cloth. I would have liked to question them about the devil-devils but had no language. That evening I asked more from my host.

"They believe that anyone who sees the devils will die soon after."

"Has anyone seen them?"

"Well, yes," he said, "the man who was here before me. He saw them."

He went on to explain, "I don't own this place; I manage it for a company. Jefferson was here for a couple of years or so. He had a Malay working for him as foreman. They had a quarrel about some woman, and the Malay stabbed him, and that was a day or two after he had seen the devil-devils."

"Did he say what they were like?"

"Like two corpses, hanging by their feet, head downwards. A little one and a big one. The big one screaming at the little one, and the little one screaming back, and flying through the tree-tops. That's what the natives think, and that's how Jefferson saw them. He didn't believe the story about dying. But he saw them all right, or said he did. Stinking corpses with flesh hanging ragged on them. A funny thing that he was killed so near after. A mere coincidence, don't you think?"

I was intrigued. Many things became different when one lived alone. I remembered how odd it had seemed in the Australian bush when I was alone all day. The old hermits that lived in the Libyan deserts had seen devils, or thought they had.

We were sitting on the veranda and a light breeze was rattling the hard leaves of the palms against one another. "You won't hear them when there is wind," said Peterson, "only when it is still, which isn't very often."

I resolved to go down to the plantation and listen at close quarters should the opportunity arise. While we were standing there the Fijian house-boy, who usually slept somewhere behind the bungalow, came panting up the slope. He had come back from Nathamaki with the message that the head men of the village would meet me on the morrow and go with me to the hilltop from whence the turtles were called.

"Did you see how scared he was?" said Peterson. "They hate going anywhere near the plantation after dark. It was all I could do to persuade him to sleep up here, and then only because he is half-brother to my wife."

"What does the name Matana mean?"

"The face."

"A queer name."

"Yes, all this district is called that. The Matana plantation."

I remembered some fragment of modern psychology I had picked up. Didn't the egg-faced men have a sinister implication? Did not veiling the face mean more than showed on the surface? And indeed no man could look upon the Face of God not even Moses.

My host was pleased to have someone to talk to. So long as we talked of shell and fish and animals, we got on well. He was a good observer, and his hobby was fishing in various forms. He reproached me for not having brought a packet of newspapers. His last knowledge of the great world dated more than a month back. I had nothing with me but the two small red volumes of George Meredith's poems, which have always been with me on all my travels. I had stupidly neglected the wants of a man cut off from his fellows. My own interest was in this large island of volcanic rock fringed with coral, with one or two flat places near the shore where coconut palm flourished.

There was another white planter who had a plantation on the
other side of the island, a ten-mile walk by the shortest route over
the foothills and through thick jungle growth. In the early days
when my host had come to Matana, they had visited once or twice.
Now they had no contact; I gathered there had been some trouble
about wives.

Next day I set out for Nathamaki with a Fijian who could
speak English. When I reached the village I found a different
reception from that of the previous day. Then I was a stranger of no
importance; today three of the elder men had come to meet me.
As I drew near they squatted on their hands and gave the ritual
acknowledgement, clapping their hands in unison and exclaiming
"Wah! Wah! Wah!" several times. I answered as best I could by
clapping my hands and saying "Vanarka! Vanarka!" After these
gestures of greeting they led the way through the village, where
they were joined by four younger men. At first we went through
jungle paths among thick scrub, but later the path climbed along
a track close to the cliff-edge. It was a six-mile walk, or there-
abouts. We went in single file, three men in front, and four
following. As we got higher on the volcanic rocks where the
vegetation was not so thick, vistas of the Koro Sea, blue and placid,
were more frequent. This small sea within the vast area of the
Pacific Ocean lay beneath us like a shining mirror. The further I
went with my native companions, the greater grew my sense of
wonder. Not only the ocean with its distant islands, but all that
was near at hand, contributed to my feeling.

Small outcrops of porphyry, tufa and obsidian had been
washed bare by the rains, and round about them in some places,
like surging water, the sensitive plants seemed about to swallow
them up. These, at our rough footfalls, collapsed, as though in
pain, their leaves closing, their petioles falling. When I looked
back on our track, I could see their slow recovery, and many
butterflies and flying beetles, bees and wasps. There were
several species of the papilio butterflies, *Papilio sarpidon* and
Papilio polymnestor and painted ladies, like those we sometimes
see in England, the common Jezebel butterfly, *Delius eucharis* and
the glorious purple mormon, *Papilio polytes*. These and many
others of types I had long known, but larger and more brightly
coloured, filled me with regret that I might not capture one or two
of them. I had no net, no killing bottles or folding papers with me.
The flowering plants equalled the butterflies in splendour:

hibiscus, aristolocheas and many varieties of bauhinias, small red blossoms that clung to earth in profusion, also the red and purple bougainvillaeas.

When we reached the summit we were met by twelve lusty young men. After the usual gestures of greeting, yangona was prepared. We drank according to custom, the shell being offered to me first. They were pleased when I cast it down with the orthodox gesture and exclamation. Nothing was hurried.

We then moved nearer the cliff-edge, which fell almost perpendicularly in a sheet of volcanic rock. The young men, standing in a group, sent their voices out over the Koro Sea. They sang, not in the modern manner, but in an ancient dialect, the actual translation of the words being unknown to them. They knew only the meaning, which might be interpreted as follows:

> Come up, oh ye turtles out of the deep.
> The great Gods command.
> Bring your wives,
> But leave your little ones in the depths.
> Answer to our voices, not to be denied.
> Come, oh ye turtles,
> Do not tarry, Come!

This was repeated. And there, sure enough, on the surface of the sea, appeared eight turtles. At that distance they looked little larger than shilling pieces. Never before had I seen more than two turtles on the surface at one time; turtles are by habit solitary reptiles, and not only were there turtles, but a corresponding number of large brown fish which I judged to be about twelve feet long. No doubt these were the turtles' wives, the little ones having been left in the depths, as commanded.

In reaction to this astonishing response, I was about to raise my hand to point at these distant creatures. It was snatched down and I was politely told that it would be unlucky, not only for myself, but for all of the singers, should the gesture be completed. I felt rebuked for what must have seemed a breach of good manners; one does not point at the opposite number in a conversation. I was in the presence of the Great Unknown. The line of distant islands of volcanic rock looked like the rim of some vast extinct volcano, sunk deep into the ocean. The sunlight poured upon the wind-touched water, and a warm soft breeze blew from sea to land. The ancestors of the singers, through unnumbered generations, had thus called to the Eternal Gods in words of a forgotten script—magical words and potent to compel reptiles and fishes to leave their natural vocations and perform ritual dances.

We stood silent while the turtles, one by one, dived back into the depths, and their wives sank out of sight.

Turtles and tortoises are odd creatures. Lately I have been assured by an intelligent friend that, should a sufferer from piles sit (not too hard) on the shell of a living tortoise, the malady can be cured. I do not say I believe, but neither do I disbelieve; I *know* associations can envelop men and animals, both tame and wild. Modern man may close his eyes to them because they fail to fit the belief that cause must precede effect. There are a-causal events and we have but to scrutinize the happenings of our own lives to be persuaded that this is so.

We took our time on the descent through those flowering meadows down to the jungle paths that closed about us. Twice we halted on the way, for the Fijians are not afflicted by the western craving for speed. There was talk and laughter and more yangona.

Having visited Nathamaki and seen the calling of the turtles, there was nothing now to keep me from returning to England except the unusual calm that enveloped the Koro Sea. Few native craft had outboard engines; the coasting and inter-island luggers depended on sail. I must stay and wait for a wind. My host assured me it would without doubt come in a day or two.

That night we sat talking late, and although the bungalow was set some distance from the plantation we could hear the strange noises that he had called "devil-devils".

"I told you they came in the calm," he said.

I was under the spell of the magic of Nathamaki and now these strange, unearthly screamings completed a sense of something quite outside ordinary experiences. We listened for a while, then I said, "I should like to be nearer, to hear more."

"You have had a twelve-mile walk. Better go to bed."

But I did not feel like going to bed. I wanted to talk, and I asked about the other white planter. Did Peterson see him often?

"Not now. I used to visit him," he said, "and he used to visit here, but not now." He paused. "Not since he's got a wife. She and Susie don't hit it off.

"You see, Thomas—that's his name—didn't somehow take up

with the native people as I do. He advertised in the papers for a white woman who would come and marry him. He got several answers, photographs, letters. He hit on one, not bad-looking, not good-looking either."

"And did she come?"

"Yes, together with a missionary from Suva to marry them. Brought her sewing machine and her sewing basket and a fair number of books—prayer books and Bibles. That was his affair, but when they came over here, and found that Susie and I were not married, her ladyship was shocked. Not that she said anything, but Susie knew."

He paused while the screams from the plantation startled the quiet of the tropical night. He went on, "She even had the brass to tackle me; said I ought to marry the girl, make an honest woman of her. I should do it for the children's sake. What was going to happen to them, when I went back to Europe? . . . all kinds of questions. As politely as I could, I told her to mind her own business. These kids that grow up on the island, they run with the kids from the village, they talk Fijian better than they talk English. Their life is here. It's a good enough place, I reckon."

I said I thought it an extremely good place. No one who had never seen Europe would ever want to leave.

"No, nor would Susie. She'll be all right. She knows I shall go one day. I give her a lot of things she would not get in the ordinary run. We understand each other." Then raising his voice, "These pious ones, with noses in the air, they think they know better."

Again after a pause while we listened to the intermittent screaming, he continued, "If she lives on the island long enough, she will change her tune. A strange place. You would find it so, if you stayed."

"I do find it so."

"You should go and visit the volcano a little way up in the mountain—an old dead volcano, its pipe brimful of water. It's worth seeing. I'll go with you," he said. "Tomorrow or the next day, that's Sunday, and I always knock off."

He told me that a scientific expedition of geologists had come out from Sydney. They had taken soundings of the water in the volcano's neck. Their line was a thousand feet long but it did not reach bottom. They let down a dredge and thought there must be a big fresh-water lake underground, far below sea level. They found there were fishes, little blind ones unlike anything they had known. Unfortunately they blew their insides out as they came up out of the deep water. The scientists explored most parts of the island, and were most interested in the volcano and its underground water. How much further it went down, they never knew.

On the agreement that we should go there on Sunday, we turned in. At various periods during the night I listened to the screaming. The next morning I went on the reef. The unusual calm gave the coral pools an extra quality; all the creatures that swam, or lurked, or merely existed in the still water seemed more intensely to communicate their mysterious lives. Waves had almost ceased to lap on rock edges, the only ripples being those made by my feet.

I had my meal up at the house and talked to Susie, and tried to make friends with the shy little boy and girl. They were as retiring as little animals, unresponsive to a stranger. Susie was an easy, adjustable companion for a lonely squatter.

That evening I sat with my host on the veranda again, he to smoke and drink his whisky and I to listen. As soon as darkness came the screaming in the plantation started. I said, "I want to go closer to see if I can distinguish the voices."

"You had better not."

"But I think I will."

"If you go, I'll come with you."

"No," said Susie, who had come to us with the coffee. "Don't you go, don't either of you go. It's not safe—just silly. Devil-devils is devil-devils . . . best left alone, that's why they are sent there, away from the people."

The night was as dark as a night can be under a clouded sky. We each carried hurricane lanterns that made shade and shine among the bushes. In the plantation they flung their rays further through cleared spaces between the palm stems. The voices were silent when we entered; I thought we were going to be disappointed.

Suddenly just overhead they broke out, the fierce indignant anger and cruelty of the one, and the whining, shrinking and complaining fear of the other. They moved slowly away among the palm crests. I could not forbear looking, but I saw nothing, not the faintest stirring of a leaf. We followed them. From another direction the voices broke out again. This time they rushed towards me, passed overhead, and fled further. Again we saw nothing. This happened more than once, producing an uncanny feeling.

"Let us go back," I said. "I didn't see anything, did you?"

"Just as well."

As we stumbled our way up the dark path to the bungalow the voices, as though triumphing in our rout, increased their demonic howling.

Susie was waiting in some anxiety and with sharp words on her tongue.

We could make nothing of it. Those noises were certainly not made by any animal, no rat or flying fox; they were human voices distorted in anger and fear. I began to look for an explanation, which grew into a theory.

At night the natives avoided this place, which was the foreigner's property, an enclave cut out from ancestral territory. Into it they projected, out of their own distresses and family tensions, the evils of cruelty and fear. I felt that if all the population of the native village were removed to some other island, the voices would no longer haunt this plantation. The noises were of true devil-devils, projections from the collective unconscious of people who lived the group life. Threatening and terrible were the sub-human voices of the persecuting devil and his counterpart.

The next day Peterson and I set out for the old volcano situated about two miles inland from Matana. A path had been cut and kept open through thick jungle scrub which formed walls of vivid fecundating vegetation on either side. This jungle was mostly of undergrowth with only a few trees that here and there supported masses of creepers falling in festoons, interlaced, struggling in and through one another. Tropical jungle is no congenial environment, and on that day of calm I found it far more disturbing than the dusty plains of Western Australia. I would have hesitated to come here alone.

If we stood still, we could hear the plants growing with little fitful jerks as some stem gave way to an upthrusting shoot, could hear the champing jaws of unseen insects that devoured those glabrous leaves. Among these light sounds, made audible by the stillness, the calm grew to be in itself something to be reckoned with. It was like a great muffler, descended from some unearthly region. The path under our feet was often a running water-way, fed by many small trickles that issued from an undergrowth, containing populations of frogs and salamanders.

The pool was of clear, black water. Fed by a waterfall, it filled the neck of the extinct volcano. The last outpourings of lava must have been of more acid and soluble rock than the enclosing basalt. These had been dissolved away, leaving what was now an empty shaft going deep into the mountain.

We were hot and perspiring from our climb, and although the pool looked a bit menacing I suggested a swim. Peterson shook his head. "Go ahead, if you like. I don't like it."

I felt it would be a waste of a climb if I did not swim in such depth of water, so I loosened my skirt and dived across the almost circular thirty-foot vent. With my hands on the further edge I could feel the basalt rock going perpendicularly down, like the sides of an artificial bathing-pool. I swam into the middle, then, exhaling gradually, let myself sink. Before going many feet down I was in water that seemed, in contrast to the warm surface, icy cold.

I have always felt tropical jungle as utterly alien to myself, and now as under the waterfall I let the warm water from above pour down over me, I felt a strangeness, almost a horror in this place. There are places that both animals and men instinctively avoid. I have felt such in the western highlands of Scotland and elsewhere, but never so strongly as in the neck of this dead volcano. I swam once more around above that fathomless depth, and as I hoisted myself up over the edge, a small red-and-black snake came out from the clump of plants that I had grasped. I had been told that there were no poisonous snakes in Fiji, but that little red-and-black snake was elegant enough to deserve to be poisonous.

We sat for a time on a log listening to the splash of the waterfall and the buzz of mosquitoes; we did not talk beyond expressing our shared feelings about the queerness of the place. "It is an odd island," said my companion. "I don't take chances. It's all right as long as I keep to the job; I get on with the natives, leave them to live as they like. I live as I do." He paused and his thoughts must have strayed back to the day of my arrival. "I wish you'd brought some papers or magazines; they keep me in touch. I like to get the news."

I assured him I would send him a packet as soon as I was back in Levuka, and I thought to myself that if I lived here, I wouldn't worry about papers so long as I got letters from time to time. I was willing, as I thought in those days, to have given up civilization, except for letters and books. In another mood, however, I knew I could not accept the natural paradise of Koro any more than Herman Melville could content himself with the Marquesas Islands and the native charms of Fayaway.

We lingered in the place, so expressive of the relics of spent energy, where water had come to take the place of white hot lava; that which had been the core of the mountain had now been laid bare, and denuded nearly to its root.

"Those fish that live down there," I said, "did you see them?"

"They were short and black, almost without scales and quite blind. Their eyes, if they had any, seemed to have withered away."

"Did the men from Sydney have any idea as to what they fed on?" I asked.

Peterson did not know, and I was left to guess that there might be some kind of vegetable life growing in the dark depths, possibly a black algae. But how did the original fish eggs get down there? Had some early reptile brought them on its feet when it came to the pool to drink? Had these hatched and survived, at first near the surface? Their descendants in the course of many generations must have worked deeper, adapting as they went. Going deeper and deeper, perhaps preyed on by creatures from above, they had reached to unplumbed depths, confirming the rule that wherever there is unoccupied space, life will come to fill the vacuum.

I was sorry when we left the splash of the waterfall and were once more enveloped in the oppressive calm, but glad when we reached the edge of the jungle where several kinds of creepers were fruiting in open sunlight. Among these were grenadillas that I knew the natives found good to eat. One species in particular was an elongated fruit, pinkish-green in colour, of the same nature but far larger than the well-known passion fruit. I picked a couple of these and offered one to my companion, but he said he seldom ate jungle fruits except bananas, pawpaws and oranges.

I had eaten one, when I noticed a patch of mould on the distal end of the second. It was only a tiny speck, and the rest of the fruit looked perfectly good. I cut it in half, and ate the better end —a rash deed that I was soon to repent.

Once clear of the jungle, we could see the Koro Sea, lying blue and silvered under a cloudless sky, an empty sea without a sail. This was not the hurricane season, so no exceptional storm was expected. Peterson rejoiced in the calm, dry weather, most favourable for drying his crop of copra. From where we stood on the foothills we could see the village to the right, clustered close to the coast, and the plantation to the left, and the bungalow at Matana standing back also on the left above the plantation. All this seemed suddenly extremely remote from England and from all those I knew. It gave a sense of aloofness. A less pleasant experience was soon to follow.

That night I was woken with so violent an attack of diarrhoea that I could only with great difficulty make my way in the darkness to the outside privy. I had no lantern, only matches that I snatched in my hurry. By their occasional glimmers I could see the seat and the flickering outlines of the hut with door swinging loose, while I vomited and strained, and crouched between the spasms, shivering and sweating. From the plantation came the howlings of the devil-devils that I could vividly imagine swinging head downwards through the tree-tops. Surely, I thought, this was punishment for my audacity in daring to encroach on their domain. Perhaps my last hour had come. I certainly felt like it.

How many hours I stayed in that horrible little hut I do not know. I must have slept short spells between my shivering fits and sweatings. When the first light of dawn came, the sounds from the plantation ceased, and, now that I could see my way, I stumbled and crawled on hands and knees back to the bungalow.

The first words I gasped out at Peterson were, "Have you got any opium?"

He looked blank and didn't think he had, but Susie said it might be worth looking amongst some old junk that Jefferson had left years ago in the tool-shed.

On a shelf were a number of bottles that filled me with hope, but they turned out to be turpentine, olive oil and lubricating oil —nothing that smelt like opium. What could I do to alleviate this affliction that had by no means spent itself, and how could any grenadilla with a small patch of mould on its far end produce such upheavals in my belly and shatter my whole being? I looked desperately round the dusty tool-shed. Under some planks leaning in one corner were some old beer bottles. One of them had a screw of paper stuffed into its mouth. Eagerly I sniffed it. Yes, it was opium in some form, nearly half a bottle full.

Back at the bungalow I poured myself out a generous tot, diluted it with water and gulped it down. The delicious warmth radiated through me. Surely opium is the most praiseworthy of drugs. The first quality is to act as a stopper to the most violent outpourings, and its following phases of relaxation are exceedingly pleasant.

I lay on my bed looking into the sympathetic and kindly brown face of my hostess. Her expression under the influence of the drug was revealed in an entrancing sweetness. It gradually faded as my body became exceptionally heavy and sunk through the bed, down, down, down, till I was in the sea, under the sea, swimming in delicious water at a fathom's depth, so cool, so green and gold around me. A beautiful young woman had me by the hand, and we glided together through the lagoon with eyes open, admiring all its wonders. It was as though this lovely woman realized all that I saw and felt. She led me at last to where two small green and gold fishes were poised motionless in the sun-illumined water, head to tail, as in the sign of Pisces. I beheld these with the utmost admiration, for they expressed to me the deepest secrets of creation. As I stayed spellbound before them, I realized I was alone, and that my fair companion had left me. This also seemed in order, that I should be *alone* with the green and gold fishes.

I must have taken a very big dose, for when I at last woke I found Susie holding a cold bandage to my forehead and rubbing my wrists. She and Peterson thought I had passed out. And now I lay deliciously at rest, wondering vaguely at the magic of modern science that can concoct such potent drugs, strong enough to withstand the devil-devils and grenadillas of Koro. What would have been my fate if that neglected beer bottle had not escaped the hazards of so many years?

My recovery was rapid and complete; it seemed to change me so that I did not now notice any oppressive quality in the calm. I had come to know the island better, and unlike Peterson, whose interest was in his trade, I was able to accept the island in all its strangeness. For the days that followed I gave myself up to exploring its various aspects, and made myself, against my inclination, go again to visit the volcano pool, braving the jungle and pausing more than once to listen to the slight, never-ceasing sounds of animal and plant activity. These masses of entangled jungle-growths breathed of timeless existence. Men and women had not chosen to live on these volcanic slopes, inhabited by sala-manders, snakes, toads, caterpillars and giant spiders that spun thick elastic webs.

Day followed day, and no sail appeared on that silent sea, no chance of leaving for the world of action. On the beach, between the village and the plantation, there was always a chance of finding some rare, unknown shell amongst the great profusion that waves had washed ashore. Cowries of all sizes, oyster shells of elaborate shapes were there, and top-shells of conical formation with bright colouring, and many bright-coloured bivalves of the *Pecten* genus. Among the predators the most conspicuous were the whelks that sometimes were as much as four inches long. Whelks are provided with a protruding proboscis with strong mandibles and radula. They gnaw a hole in the shell of their victim and then thrust in the proboscis, extracting the living juices. Many of the shells on the beach had such holes bored in them, small holes in the little shells made by small whelks, and larger holes in the larger, tougher shells. Chitons, slug-shaped with eight plates, were far larger than the small chitons found at low tides on English coasts. Among the top-shells were a few sethi shells which can grow to as much as five inches across the base. These on many of the islands were sought by beachcombers and sold at that time for about a hundred pounds a ton. Out of the strong, hard columellas, pearl-shell studs and buttons are made. Time passed easily as I turned over the debris that the tides washed up. Among these accumulated harvests of past years were shells painted like sunsets or mottled like strato-cumulus clouds. Here they lay gathered together with no eyes to admire their diffuse and lovely patterns. For what purpose was this artistry? I could hardly imagine that the eyes of a snail could measure the beauty of another snail. Were they waiting for human senses to recognize these intricate patterns?

Thus I would spend the hours, then take my swim and return to the bungalow to find the ever-obliging Susie ready to prepare some kind of meal. There were no set meal-times, and only rarely did Peterson and myself chance to meet on our daytime visits to the bungalow. Susie was pleased at having a visitor. She liked to talk, and showed great interest in my collections of shells and opercula. These latter, she said, made good necklaces or, when fitted with wire, ear-rings.

When I had tired of looking for shells on the beach I would go on the reef at low tide and watch with wonder the living creatures in the coral pools and in the gullies between coral growths, where currents of well-oxygenated water were always washing to and fro. Here quite different creatures lived, and here I fished for prawns and sometimes caught a stump-tailed lobster. Each single coral pool exhibited a congregation of creatures all intent on getting their living, devouring and being devoured, yet as a whole, despite the internecine strife, presenting a sense of great harmony. I could watch the cowries browsing on sponges and sea squirts. Each knob of protruding coral had, on close inspection, its population of sea-worms, tiny polyps, tiny spider-crabs, sea-shrimps and finely divided red seaweeds. When a stone or lump of coral was detachable, I found on the underside new kinds of active life, small sea anemones and clusters of eggs waiting to hatch. Dahlia and plume anemones clung to the backs of hermit crabs or to whelk shells. Sometimes I came on colonies of long-stemmed hydra that looked like miniature waving forests, having instead of tree-tops outstretched tentacles.

Once, and only once, I came on a living file-shell that had detached itself from its usual hiding place and gone for a swim. The bivalve shell of delicate pinks was surrounded and partly hidden by a web-work of extruded tentacles, of blended orange and pale scarlet. It swam in an upright position by slowly opening and half shutting its valves. I had found many of these dead shells washed up on the beach, but only once saw the living creature taking its pleasure in its native element.

Such were a few of the things that the calm revealed. Also, there were star-fish and sea-urchins with long spikes within whose protection certain small fishes took refuge. Among the numerous fine-branching corals of the pools swam small brilliant-coloured fishes. These things I had seen in hurried glimpses through the glass-bottomed bucket as I had been rowed along the coast of Moturiki, but now, with the water's surface stilled by the prevailing calm, they were revealed in detail to a more leisured look. From coral fronds groups of pipe-fish appeared like the clustered snakes on a Medusa's head.

Although part of me fretted for the calm to end, this life of sea and reef made me feel how pleasant it would be to live like the lotus eaters and forgo the strife and tumult of existence, remaining on this small strip of island-shore with its natural wonders coexisting in convincing harmony. Yet in this seductive landscape were also the decomposing corpses that ranged on still nights through the palm-crests of Matana, the Place of the Face.

SIX

The Return

ON THE SIXTEENTH DAY of my stay on Koro the calm broke. A freshening breeze came from the east and before long a sail appeared, which was vigorously hailed. An overcrowded pearling lugger, or rather one that had been used for pearling, dropped her sails and tied up alongside the jetty. There was a great deal of talking which I could not follow. I was introduced to the owner of the boat, and it was agreed that he was to take me to Levuka for the sum of ten shillings. This may seem a mean sum for a passage, but ten shillings at that time was in value about four pounds of our present currency, and was not considered unreasonable. I readily agreed, and after I had said my farewells to Peterson and Susie, I went aboard with my knapsack and two linen bags full of shells. Having had some experience of native boats I took up a position in the bows, and hoped for a speedy passage. Little did I guess that for more than four days and nights I was destined to be associated with that highly-smelling, over-crowded lugger. Boats that had once carried pearl-shell always retained the stench of decomposing fish, and mixed with the aroma of copra that had also been a cargo, it was enough to decide me that however uncomfortable it might be to curl up with the anchor, there was at least likely to be a breeze in this forward situation.

We pushed off with mutual salutations and farewells, and sail was set. Before long I noticed that instead of making with a beam-wind southeast towards Levuka, we were going westward with main-sheet fully extended. By this time I had become familiar with a few necessary Fijian phrases, and I went aft to expostulate with the owner, who was seated at the tiller. "Levuka, Levuka!" I said, pointing in the direction of that not-so-distant isle.

"Mar-lo-wa, Mar-lo-wa," he responded, and that was about all I could get out of him. "Mar-lo-wa", which means "by and by", is a much used phrase amongst Fijians.

The captain was perfectly polite, but firm in his resistance to my suggestion that he was going in the wrong direction. Had he been going to Levuka we could have made the passage in about eight hours. As it was, we sailed all night westward. The wind did not abate, but rather increased. The bows from time to time plunged into the waves, drenching me with spray.

An evening meal was announced of the usual fare provided on small boats—snapper, boiled in salt water, yam and ndalo roots. For me it was indeed a "humble pie"; I was quite helpless, knew not whither I was going, and was internally seething with indignation tempered with an increasing uneasiness, which grew as night came swiftly. We continued to bowl along into the dark unknown. Under other circumstances it would have been an exhilarating experience—the foam-capped waves, sometimes bearing streaks of phosphorescence, the delightful splashing of water, and the not unpleasant capfuls of warm spray that from time to time came aboard.

A courteous Fijian suggested that I should go down into the cabin amidst the unknown number of women and children. My wonder was that so many human beings could have squeezed into so small a space. Considering what I knew of the smells of one-time pearl luggers, I thought it best to refuse, and say I could quite well do as I was.

These were words easier said than realized, for I was sleepy and thought if I should go deep asleep I might easily be washed overboard. The anchor was my only consolation, both pillow and bedfellow. I coiled myself around it, and tying my bags and knapsack together made the best of my position. By no means a comfortable night, it was not altogether to be regretted, for I found one position in which I could lie and look up at the stars as they raced round each time the boat plunged before the following wind.

The supreme beauty of the dawn made me feel that the opportunity to experience such loveliness was well worth the discomforts of the night. The sun came up behind us, its crimson rays slipping over the white foam of the waves. The slanting light danced over the sea behind us in the red glare, and forward where in the middle distance palm trees seemed to be raising their glistening crowns from a shore as yet invisible. This was my first sight of a coral atoll as described by Darwin in his *Journal of a Voyage Round the World*. As we came nearer I could see the outline of the string of coral islets, like the near-circular patterns made by fungi on grass. We passed close to the reef with both main and lug-sails still filled with the breeze, now considerably abated. This atoll appeared to be uninhabited by human beings, though it was no doubt often visited for the collection of nuts. Shortly after passing the atoll we turned southwards, and by shortening sail a more pleasant movement was given to the boat. At this angle the wind came fresh from the sea, uncontaminated by odours of rotten fish.

It was about noon that we came close inshore to a small volcanic island with its inevitable fringing reef. We negotiated the passage and tied up at a small jetty in the lagoon. Here we all disembarked, and I was glad to stretch my legs. I did not at first realize that this was a leper island. No doubt our visit would not have been authorized by the government, but several of our crew were visiting relatives. We all went to the village, and only gradually did it dawn on me that most of the islanders bore marks of the dreaded disease.

Well, if my companions took the risk, so must I. Without showing too obvious signs of keeping to myself. I took what precautions I could. By this time I had tired of expostulating and repeating "Levuka", though I determined that I would report these deceivers and law-breakers as soon as I did ultimately land on Ovalau.

Striving to be as polite as my hosts, I stayed in their company for a while, then sloped off by myself to the beach, where I found one or two shells that I had not seen before. I was also interested in the sea birds: two kinds of tern, a fork-tailed hawk-like bird, and the usual company of gulls and gannets. I did not stray far, for I must keep an eye on the owners of the lugger and return with them. I did not want to be left on the leper island.

As dusk drew on it became obvious that they were spending the night. I decided to sleep on the beach and defy the inquisitive probings of crabs. When one is young sleep comes naturally, and although the sand was damp I slept well, though I was a little cold at first dawn.

After a meal we returned to the lugger; again I repeated my parrot-call of "Levuka, Levuka", and again I was answered by "Mar-lo-wa". Once more we sailed southward, and before long landed on another island, this time not populated by lepers. I was growing accustomed to this unsolicited adventure; it was offering a good ten shillings' worth. I did my best to talk to the natives, and on this island ate and drank with better zest and firmer confidence. The milk of young coconuts would in any case be free of infection. We spent another night ashore, and this time I slept amongst the men on the matted floor of one of the houses. Before leaving I joined in the ceremonial drinking of yangona.

On board again, we began slow wide tacks against the prevailing east wind. My host now smilingly assured me we were heading for Levuka. We sailed all through the day and following night. Again I was invited to the cabin, but could not face it. All those women and children with their pots of urine were too much for my artificial sensibilities. Once more I would have to embrace the anchor and make the best of the water that continually splashed on board. This was the most miserable night of all, and I would have paid many shillings to avoid it. Dawn came at last, and with it the distant sight of Ovalau. My mood now became morose and I did not respond to the smiling gesture of my host as he named the landfall.

I think he must have guessed that I was likely to make some complaint to the British Consul at Levuka. At a small hamlet, owning its own jetty, he intimated I might land, making it clear that I had only to follow the coastal path and I would soon be at Levuka. I accepted his proposal, eager to be quit of that boat. My wet knapsack and my bags of shells were a considerable burden, and the path, often traversing the jungle, was none too easy to follow. Before I had travelled that four miles, punctuated by several stops to rest and find easier positions for my burdens, the wily captain of the lugger had had plenty of time to call at Levuka, do what business he needed, and again set sail.

Any thoughts of vengeance soon dispersed. It was better thus; he had saved me making myself unpleasant, and after all, I had seen atolls in their pristine glory, visited a leper island and learned how to sleep with an anchor for a bedfellow, and here I was with Englishmen to listen to my grievances, at which they laughed. They took me to the white man's club house, where I had a delicious hot bath, and spent two days and nights rehabilitating myself before returning to Suva, up the Rewa river. Here I would find again all the comforts of civilization.

The town of Suva with mountains behind and mud flats in front is well designed to capture and hold the heat of tropical summers. My return from Koro was in January, which in the southern hemisphere is the height of the hottest weather. The temperature in Suva—96° Fahrenheit during the dark hours—was far more oppressive than the dry climate of Bernier Island when the thermometer registered 115° in the shade at noon. I found it as hot as the steam room of a Turkish bath, and having returned from my enforced stay on the island, which was very much cooler, I wished I was back again.

I was uncertain what to do. There was a chance that I might still go with the Lord Chief Justice to the Windward Islands, and I thought I should not miss such an opportunity. However, there would be a delay, and against this plan I felt a strong pull to return to England. I was short of money; this also was a consideration. I must keep my fare for the homeward journey, and how was it possible to make money in Suva?

I was put up at the club and there I could lodge for some days at any rate, but in great discomfort from the stuffy, oppressive heat and the swarm of mosquitoes that could not be excluded by fly-proof window frames. In my bedroom their zooming wings completely shut out any sight of the ceiling. I had of course a mosquito net, under whose tent I could crawl and lie naked on my bed to watch the mosquitoes settling on the outside, hungry for human blood. Inevitably one or two would get through, and then the exertion of trying to kill them would produce a profuse sweat. In the morning two or three would be pitched on the inside of the net, swollen red with my blood.

In the heat it was difficult to sleep. As soon as I dropped off the fact of relaxation would swell the peripheral veins and I would wake in a sweat. I was lucky in having a bath in my room. It was built into the floor, four feet square, and I could squat in the tepid water with just my head out. This was slightly cooling, but the effort of drying would inevitably produce a flushed feeling and pulsing in the ears.

Still undecided whether to stay or go, I was offered a well-paid job to supervise the emptying of the earth closets in a certain quarter of the town. This did not appeal to my pampered taste. Not that I should have had to empty any buckets myself, but I did not fancy myself as a minor boss of indentured Indian labour.

While I was looking around and considering, two nightmare occurrences prevented any movement. The first hypnotized me, the second laid me on on my back with a fever. The first of these events was a huge flight of butterflies which descended on the town. They came into Suva Bay from over the sea, from the direction of Valu Levu. I think, though I cannot be certain, that they were of the species *Papilio crina*. Each insect in this swarm might well be considered beautiful as an individual. Dark blue and black, its velvety wings with serrated margins stretched to nearly three inches when expanded. Its movement was a graceful lilting flight, but in a thick swarm they produced in the human mind something akin to horror. The insects filled the lower stratum of the air with their flutterings, and when they perched, covered the ground. Horses' hooves in the streets crushed and slid on them, wheels skidded, and soon bands of coolies were employed sweeping the dead bodies away. They perched on bushes, trees, houses, on chairs and tables, on windows and doors, and on the clothes of humans, and on faces and hands, if not constantly brushed off. In no place out of doors could one be free of them. Stretched on a deck chair in the oppressive heat, I have looked at my legs and arms covered all over with velvety blue and black wings, each pair pulsating with its peculiar and insistent ecstasy. They became, in their overwhelming, collective vitality, repulsive to sight and imagination. If I closed my eyes I could still hear the snap and rustle of wings, still see the opening and shutting of blue and black under the shadow of my eyelids. They became a distorted fancy, not belonging to the world of sane actuality, but rather a feverish manifestation of disquiet. They conjured up the illusion that all things the senses perceived were infected by their movement. From time to time each butterfly would lift its tail to emit a globule of claret-coloured excrement. No action, however brutal, could frighten them. When brushed away, or crippled by a blow, they would lie where they fell, their squelchy bodies and brittle wings combining softness and stiffness in a peculiarly repulsive manner. The dead and dying lay every-where, squashed in thousands, emitting a pungent odour. Many were mutilated and held by their congealing juices. On the dead and dying the living perched, and never ceased the rhythmic play of lifting and depressing their wings, expressing the blind drive from which human reason recoils.

From the jungles on the encompassing hillsides, where tangles of vegetation were increasing at tropical speed, the butterflies had come, and now they covered with their shimmering blues and blacks the comparatively small area that human ingenuity had made for itself. They seemed to embody a potent and fecund life that would prevail in jungles when man was no more. They forced themselves on our sight, and like sexual images on Hindu temples, attracted while they repelled. I looked at them with fascination.

I thought of the bushes, somewhere in the jungle, that their caterpillars had stripped bare, and of all the empty pupa cases hanging by their tails. Why had they gathered here where no suitable plants grew on which they could lay their eggs? As I watched them I discovered that they were all males; no single female could I see anywhere. These superfluous bachelors were an enigma comparable with the multitude of desiccated ticks that I had seen in the Australian bush hanging by two of their eight legs, withered and scorched to death by the sun's heat.

On the hundreds of thousands of dead butterflies that were strewn everywhere, correspondingly large hosts of scavengers were gathering for the feast. Birds did not eat these butterflies, but smaller creatures were not so fastidious. The red ants in vast numbers devoured the dead and the crippled. They made labyrinths within those succulent bodies, approaching and retreating in long, fine lines, making networks among the corpses. Large forest-ants, cockroaches and beetles of all kinds tore with hungry mandibles at the soft flesh, and hornets and wasps and many small-winged flies came for their share. The feast was uninterrupted even during the night hours. As soon as the sun was up, further flocks of newly-emerged butterflies descended on the town, unfolding and up-jerking their wings in salutation to the life that laid them low.

For four days the butterflies continued to come out of the jungles into the open spaces of the town. Their numbers appeared undiminished until noon of the fourth day when their cloud lifted, the sky was darkened, and on a rising wind it swept over the bay towards the western hills, leaving a few of their number fluttering in a disconsolate manner over the squashed fragments of the dead and dying. Soon the scavengers had finished their clearing-up operations, and the armies of ants were, by the end of the day, withdrawing, leaving a fine dust to be blown away on the wind.

With the departure of the butterflies I experienced great relief; the mescal dream was no more; the world of man's activities took on its normal character A slight breeze had come, and the nights were not quite so hot. At the club I met a Fijian chieftain who suggested I should go on horseback with him into the hilly country of the interior. I was not feeling very well, but I did not like to refuse. He provided me with a spirited-looking animal. "He pulls a bit," he said, "but I suppose you can ride?" I supposed I could, as I had had some experience of difficult horses both in England and Australia.

The first part of our journey was pleasant enough. My companion spoke fluent English, but I became aware, as we rode on together, that he had a certain toughness which could easily develop into the cruelty that had supported cannibalistic customs in past times.

It was a long ride, longer than I wished for, and as time passed I felt increasingly unwell. But this was not to be mentioned. When at last we turned back, the road sloped gently down hill, descending with many turnings. He suggested that we have "a bit of a canter", and it was not for me to object. The canter soon became a gallop. The wily Fijian, who was out to test my horsemanship, fell behind a little but not for long. He increased his pace trying to overtake me, as indeed he soon did on his excellent mount. My own horse that, as he had said, was a bit of a puller, did not like being passed, and our gallop soon became a wild race along a downward slope.

He gave me a long, rough ride, and not only once but several times he fell behind and then overtook me. By the time we reached Suva I was completely done in. My Fijian regarded me with some satisfaction, and no doubt thought me a feeble creature. I made the best of my condition, thanked my companion and, seeking to control my trembling limbs, went back to the club for a bath and then to bed. Here I stayed for several days with what Dr. Fox, who attended me, called dengue fever. I do not think it was the *pukka* variety, but something like it. Anyway I felt very ill and no doubt the rough ride had not improved my resistance. I remembered little of this time except that butterflies' wings in constant movement haunted my fever-dreams.

The delay caused by my fever had ruled out the possibility of an excursion to the Windward Islands. While I was convalescing at the club and watching with some anxiety the dwindling of my funds, I received a cable from England making my return imperative.

S.S. *Marama* was an old boat of ill reputation on account of the rotten bilge-water in her keel which gave its aroma to all the lower deck cabins. She was the first boat bound for Vancouver and I was lucky to secure a berth. Since I had to travel at a cheap rate, the state-room for which I had a ticket had four berths, and five men had paid for a passage in it. Its only means of ventilation led into a passage deep in the ship, the door of which opened opposite the men's lavatory. Although I had a ticket for a berth and the fifth man had not, I decided that I would sleep on deck. Selfishly, I claimed the mattress, which I rolled up, and left the empty berth to the other claimant to make the best he could of it. All the cheaper cabins were booked to overflowing.

When most people had turned in for the night I unrolled the mattress and wrapped myself in my tapa. The nights were warm and pleasant and the sea moderate, but I had to rise early when sailors came at the first streak of dawn to wash down the decks. Then I could climb on to one of the hatchways where my position was neither secure nor comfortable.

Early on this voyage I made the acquaintance of a young man of about my own age; we met where a rope separated the first from the second-class passengers. He had, shortly before embarking, come from New Zealand on a small steamer calling at some of the Kermadec and Tonga Islands. We compared our travelling experiences; his were those of a rich young Englishman, mine of a penniless beachcomber. We hit it off well together, and he soon suggested that I should put my leg over the rope and join him on the upper deck reserved for first-class passengers. "If the steward says anything to you, leave it to me, I'll fix it," he said. Half sovereigns placed at the right time into the right palms can work most things on board ship. So it was that I spent much time on the upper deck with my new friend. I had to go back to the second-class saloon for meals, and so long as the weather kept fine, I was content to spend my nights on deck, to fall asleep lulled by a happy consciousness of the throbbing presence of the ship and all its human activities, and glad to have the sky above me that ever seemed both familiar and remote. I was happy in the thought that I was returning home after so many months.

I forget how many days the passage to Hawaii took, but I shall not forget the beauty of the scene as we entered the harbour, nor the blue shark that came and displayed itself by the side of our stationary ship while preparations were being made for the landing party. With the sunrise the sea's surface glittered with tiny sparks, as instantaneously lost as found. This sparkle, which is the same wherever sunlight falls on waves, can produce after a time a mesmeric effect, holding the glance on the surface, yet at times tempting the sight through to the clear deeps beneath. While I was idly watching, there rose slowly the torpedo shape of a blue shark. As it surfaced it turned its fifteen-foot length of body on its side, then on its back, as it glided a few inches beneath the wavelets. It exposed its slanting eye-slits, its gill-openings, its turned-down mouth with large spongy proboscis, and the paler tints of its belly. As it passed it belched up a bubble of air, then slid leisurely into the deeps, its proper home. It had risen for its own obscure purpose, but this revelation thrilled me, for in the horror of its form was contained part of the enchantment of the sea.

At Hawaii I went ashore with my new companion. This island was different from Koro and Suva, with a beauty peculiarly its own. At that time there were a great many waterways amongst green meadows between the sea and the town. White birds floated on these blue strips where the brilliance of the sky found reflection. The town itself was delightful, especially the Japanese in national costume, and so also were their houses, which looked to be built of paper.

After having indulged in the exceptional ice-creams served by Japanese girls, we went to the Aquarium, the best that I had ever seen or hope to see. Here I could watch again and recognize some of the creatures of the rock pools, and in the deeper tanks were sea fishes, octopus, squids and enormous eels. Here I learned the names of creatures that I had seen in the rock pools.

The *Marama* was not to sail till eight o'clock that evening. We had the day before us. My companion insisted on standing lunch in a Japanese restaurant, and afterwards we took a tram to some place recommended in the guide book. We passed many trees covered in scarlet blossoms but bearing no leaves. Leaving the tram, we walked a mile or so to a pleasant promontory that overlooked the bay. My companion told me of his journey from New Zealand in a small coasting steamer of about four hundred tons. The first-class state rooms were all on the upper deck, placed so that they opened into the central saloon. He had one to himself, but soon noticed that in the next state room was someone with heavy stertorous breathing, and so also on the other side. At the first meal-time he looked out for these gentlemen, but could by no means identify them. There were only a few first-class passengers, men and women of refined appearance.

When he returned to his state room he listened attentively. Yes, there was the deep, slow breathing, as if the occupant was suffering from some chest complaint. Disturbed and a bit worried by the noise, he knocked but received no answer. That night he asked the steward about the occupants of the adjacent rooms. He received an evasive reply. He listened and watched, but neither that day not the next did he see the occupants of either room. He noticed however a peculiar sweetish smell, and both night and day the sighing went on, a sad exhalation. Soon all the passengers were talking about these mysterious breathings that came from several of the state rooms, and now that the ship was at sea and well on her way, the secret could no longer be kept. Since the ship was filled with cargo under the hatches, the cabins had been used to give accommodation to living turtles, destined to be made into soup. These reptiles would travel more conveniently alive than dead, and since they were almost impossible to kill anyway, they had been wedged into the empty state rooms.

The aroma that issued from them was not too bad till the ship ran into heavy weather. Then the normal reptilian breathings were replaced by retchings, for the turtles were being sea-sick. Accustomed to the movements of surface waves, they did not adjust to the rolling and pitching of a small steamship. When in bad weather the latches were battened down the stench was wellnigh intolerable. "However," he said with a smile, "one can get accustomed to almost anything."

As the old *Marama* pitched and rolled her way northward, we ran into colder weather. I found my tapa wrapping was no longer sufficient to keep me warm. I confided to my friend my dilemma of either being exposed to the increasing cold, or finding haphazard moments of sleep in one of the corridors, being constantly stepped-over by other passengers as they made their way to the W.C. and urinals. He generously offered me the couch in his very superior state room. Each night I crept unostentatiously into a forbidden and unpaid-for luxury. No one was a penny the worse.

At Vancouver I parted from my good friend and though, after fifty years, I have forgotten his name, I still feel a gratitude for the cosy nights I spent in his cabin. Ours was an altogether chaste relationship, indeed no homosexual thoughts ever entered our minds—not until the day we left the ship did I catch in the eye of his steward the shadow of a suspicion.

I stayed one day and two nights in Vancouver. I suspected there had been some heavy rainfalls, for many of the streets were deep in mud, and without duckboards it would not have been possible to walk where pavements should have been. The city appeared primitive in comparison with Sydney.

I had to keep careful watch on my money, for although I had a ticket that would carry me through to Liverpool, there would be expenses on the long journey across the continent; and since I had heard so much about the grandeur of the Rocky Mountains, I determined to break the journey at Banff. I could afford to wait two days at Vancouver; these I spent walking in the woodlands that were not far from the city. Two species of squirrels were very common, one bushy-tailed which I assumed to be the Adijedono of Longfellow's "Hiawatha," the other was like a small orange-coloured lizard, and, like a lizard, clung close to the tree stems as it ran. I did not go very far, for I constantly met notices saying *KEEP OUT* or *AVOID TROUBLE—THIS MEANS YOU.* Such menacing unfriendliness I took to be the attitude of this country towards strangers. I kept out, and in my short conversations with the native Canadians, I had the same feeling. The white Australians had been considered generally hostile to Englishmen, rough in speech and manner, but they were positively courteous in comparison with the Canadians. Perhaps I was unfortunate, and the fact that I was so deeply sun-tanned as to be easily mistaken for a Coloured may have accounted for my rough reception. With little regret I left Vancouver for the adventure of the rail journey.

The rail-track followed a river between mountains on each side. At first this was an exciting outlook, but soon the endless fir forests became monotonous, though sometimes as the train emerged from sheltered ways that still held back the winter's snow, exciting vistas down steep declivities to distant river-beds came up fully to my anticipation. The food on the Canadian Pacific Railroad I found extravagantly priced, and I soon realized that I would have to eat very little.

At Banff I stayed for twenty-four hours, and found this quite long enough. Perhaps it was the season that gave to the scenery so gloomy an aspect. Bare, hideous upheavals of rock, with here and there a scrubby moss-like covering of pine trees, divided by sprawled glaciers covered with moraine, afforded a dismal contrast to the remembered beauty of the Blue Mountains, and the volcanic peaks of Fiji. It may well be that I offered a scruffy appearance myself, since my clothes were none too clean and I probably looked half-starved. What did fill me with admiration was the fire in the station waiting-room, which must have covered a good sixty feet in area. It could take a cartful of six-foot logs at one loading. It was a joy to watch the flames of this roaring blaze keeping humans warm against the outer frost.

By the time our train reached Winnipeg I was doubtful whether I could keep body and soul together on the long stretch across the plains to Montreal. During the hour's wait, I went into the town to forage, and found an eating house that provided an excellent meal at a moderate price. With forethought I bought two boxes of grapenuts, and on these, moistened with water, I lived for the three and a half days' journey to Montreal.

I looked out for the prairie-dogs as we went across the great flat stretches of steppe land. The country nearer the coast, with lakes, forests and rivers, was more attractive, but still monotonous, and grapenuts and water were not the best of food to stimulate aesthetic appreciation. I listened to the gossip on the train which was packed to full capacity; I had been lucky to get a seat. The talk was that the steamers going to England would all be booked up. Although I held a ticket, this did not guarantee a berth as well, and I would not be allowed to embark without a berth. I certainly would not be the only one to apply for a last-minute vacancy. Hampered as I was with fourteen pieces of luggage, I was likely to be some time clearing the customs.

As soon as we pulled up at Montreal station, I abandoned my luggage, and seeing an empty train in the opposite siding, I ducked under the couplings between two coaches, ran along the far side, wriggled through a hole in the fence, and hurried down

to the shipping office. Yes, two berth tickets had been returned.
I secured one of them and leisurely strolled back to meet a crowd
surging post haste to the shipping office.

My luggage was as I had left it, all but my guncase which
someone had walked off with. I lost a good gun together with
several treasures packed in some of the small compartments.
However I could not expect to get through without losses, and
what would I have done had I been left in an expensive colonial
town without any money?

When safely on board I experienced a great feeling of elation
and I felt it was not wrong that I should be coming home after so
many adventures with but little more than three pounds in my
possession. I had seen quite a lot of the world. I was not in debt,
and I had just enough to tip the stewards. And now there was the
voyage to look forward to.

Unexpectedly, there was an additional loveliness to be added
to my memories. Near the mouth of the St. Lawrence river we
encountered mist and icebergs drifting southwards from the
glaciers of Newfoundland. We went dead slow, and I could watch
several fantastically shaped icebergs come drifting out of the mist,
their silver, black and white surfaces illuminated by a faint
sunlight struggling from the pearl-coloured sky above.

I arrived in Liverpool with one sovereign and a few loose
shillings in my pocket.

How polite the English people seemed in contrast to the
Canadians. Never till now had I realized how much I loved my
native land. Life appeared richer, more splendid than when I set
out. If there had been magic in the South Seas, there was also a
potent charm in a tuft of grass sprouting in springtime green
beside a muddy pavement—it brought tears to my eyes.

I set out for the house of Mr. Brown, a schoolmaster. He and
his beautiful young wife received me with enthusiasm. I had
known them at Cambridge, and they welcomed me now, bearded
and tanned, as a man from another hemisphere. I could stay as
long as I liked and would I tell his boys about the aborigines of
Western Australia: a formal lecture on Saturday evening for
which I would receive a fee of five pounds.

PRINTED IN GREAT BRITAIN BY
WESTERN PRINTING SERVICES LTD., BRISTOL